Women's Clubs of Denver

D1096084

Essays in Colorado History

NUMBER 13
1992

Women's Clubs of Denver
is a regular issue of *Essays
in Colorado History*
consisting of two related
studies of Denver women's
clubs from the 1880s to the
middle of the twentieth
century.

COLORADO
HISTORICAL
SOCIETY

Essays in Colorado History
ISSN 1046-3119

Editor
David N. Wetzel

Assistant Editor
Clark Secrest

Book Review Editor
David Fridtjof Halaas

Editorial Intern
Catherine Morris

Design and Production
Laetitia Lawler
Susan Romansky

Publications Assistant
Joseph Dean

The Colorado Historical Society publishes *Essays and Monographs in Colorado History* (ISSN 0899-0409) periodically to provided a flexible scholarly forum for well-written, documented manuscripts on the history of Colorado and the Rocky Mountain West. Its twofold structure is designed to accommodate article-length manuscripts in the traditional journal style and longer, book-length works which appear as separate monographs within the series. Volumes of *Essays in Colorado History* (ISSN 1046-3119) are numbered consecutively and indexed every five years. *Monographs in Colorado History* (ISSN 1046-3100) carries its own numbering system, and each volume is individually indexed. The publications of the Society generally follow the principles and conventions of the *Chicago Manual of Style,* and an author's guide is available upon request. Manuscripts and queries should be addressed to: Publications Office, Colorado Historical Society, 1300 Broadway, Denver CO 80203. The Colorado Historical Society disclaims responsibility for statements of fact or opinion made by contributors.

CONTENTS

Gail M. Beaton
The Widening Sphere
of Women's Lives:
The Literary Study and
Philanthropic Work of
Six Women's Clubs in
Denver, 1881–1945   1

Lynda F. Dickson
Lifting as We Climb:
African-American Women's
Clubs of Denver, 1890–1925   69

Appendix   99

Index   105

Cover: Colorado Federation of Women's
Clubs luncheon brings clubwomen
together in the late 1940s. *Western History
Department, Denver Public Library*

Gail M. Beaton

The Widening Sphere of Women's Lives

The Literary Study and Philanthropic Work of Six Women's Clubs in Denver, 1881–1945

About the author
Gail M. Beaton received her B.S. degree in education from the University of Colorado at Boulder and in 1987 was awarded an M.A. degree in history from the University of Colorado at Denver. This article has been developed from her master's thesis.

INTRODUCTION

T HE WOMEN'S CLUB movement in the United States was initiated in 1868 by journalist Jane Cunningham Croly (Jennie June), who founded the Sorosis Club in New York City, and by reformer Caroline Severance, who founded the New England Woman's Club in Boston.[1] Between 1868 and 1900, white middle- and upper-class women banded together to form women's clubs in cities across the nation.[2] In 1890 Jane Croly called upon the clubwomen to form a national organization of women's clubs for the benefit of all. In April they organized the General Federation of Women's Clubs to "bring into communication with each other the various clubs throughout the world, in order that they may compare methods of work and become mutually helpful."[3] By the height of the Progressive era in 1914, the General Federation had grown to a membership of nearly two million American women who were active on many committees of reform and philanthropy, such as legislation, public health, conservation, household economics, civil service, and child labor.[4]

In the beginning, however, women's groups were not politically active. The first women's literary clubs arose primarily for intellectual stimulation. The women studied classical literature, languages, history, and art. The clubs became, in Croly's words, "middle-aged women's universities."[5] Members held meetings weekly or biweekly for two hours in the evening or afternoon between October and June. These months, when school was in session, allowed the women the opportunity to meet free of immediate motherly duties. There were no club meetings or activities in the summer because some families left town for extended vacations.[6] To join, a candidate had to be sponsored by two or more members and approved by a large percentage of the executive committee or by the entire club. Because most sponsors informally sounded out other members before a nomination, rarely was a candidate rejected for membership.[7]

In the early years, criticism was often directed at the clubs for supporting woman suffrage, and to avoid this charge, many adopted innocuous or nonpolitical names—based, for example, on the day of the week on which the club met, or on fruit-bearing flowers, neighborhoods, or allusions to classical and literary figures—and forbade discussion of suffrage and religion.[8] A city library was usually the first project the clubwomen became involved in, often in answer to their own need for books to read for club papers and discussions.[9]

During the 1870s and 1880s, however, several clubs began studying the living and working conditions of the poor, the public and private charities organized to help them, and laws concerning women. From this effort, clubwomen developed a permanent concern for the poor and the need for reform legislation. With the organization of the General Federation in 1890, the work of the women's literary clubs embraced the causes of reform, and philanthropy became a permanent part of all club work. Newer organizations were formed, known as "departmental clubs," which stressed philanthropy rather than literary arts, as had the older clubs of the 1870s and 1880s. By the 1890s the club movement accommodated both efforts within an organizational structure that consisted of permanent committees or departments, each of which chose themes or projects on which to work. The individual clubs then adapted national and state projects to the specific needs of their own communities.[10]

But it was the early literary study and discussions which had laid the foundation for all that followed. The literary clubs introduced a sense of sisterhood and increased self-confidence in public speaking, in researching, and in writing skills that enabled the women to forge ahead. The leaders of the General Federation encouraged all member clubs to pursue some form of philanthropic project among the poor in their communities and to lobby for the passage of all kinds of reform legislation in their state legislatures.

The reform spirit flourished in the federation and its member clubs from 1890 to 1914. At that point, the first World War brought new problems and concerns for clubwomen. For the next thirty years, events in the nation and the world demanded more of the clubwomen's efforts. Shifting their priorities, they supported the war effort in two wars through work with the Red Cross, bond sales, canteens, conservation, and military hospitals. Where there was a need, a club or clubwoman was ready to answer the call to service. The same was true during the Great Depression. Even though many of the women and their families, like other Americans, were hurt by the Depression, they tried to help those less fortunate than themselves. And, although inundated by community projects, many clubs continued their literary studies and presentations of papers. The needs of the world, the nation, and the community altered—but did not end—many of the original objectives of the clubs.

In Colorado, the pattern of the woman's club was much the same as the rest of the nation. However, because the state itself was so young, the first woman's clubs did not appear until the early 1880s. In Denver, among white women, the Fortnightly Club and the Monday Literary Club were the first organize. In subsequent years, these two were joined by other women's clubs, including the Clio, Reviewers, Woman's Club, Round Table, Twenty-Second Avenue Study, North Side Woman's, Sphinx, and Tuesday Morning Class.[11] In 1895 the four oldest clubs—the Fortnightly, Monday Literary, Round Table, and Clio—and the rapidly growing Woman's Club issued the call to others in the state to organize a state federation.[12] Although many of these clubs were already members of the General Federation, the organization of the Colorado Federation of Women's Clubs brought greater cooperation among the state clubs. It offered more opportunities for personal leadership, more effective lobbying efforts, and greater visibility and publicity for the clubs and their leaders. By 1899 the 108 Colorado federated clubs and their 4,700 members were participating in committee work in education, traveling libraries, music, art, school legislation, and the preservation and restoration of prehistoric ruins in southwestern Colorado.[13]

Through the Progressive era, the Colorado women's clubs labored for a wide variety of reforms at the local, state, and national levels in matters of health, public hygiene, education, and sensible fashions. One famous clubwoman, Dr. Florence R. Sabin, was instrumental in the successful fight for what are now known as the Sabin health laws in the state of Colorado.

The welfare of women and children was a special concern of the women's club movement in the United States, and Colorado was no exception. Not only did club members lobby strongly for mother's compensation, an eight-hour workday for women, and the child labor amendment, but they also supported pensions for the blind, the Workshop for the Adult Blind, and equal pay for equal work. For the youth of the state, the Colorado federated clubs achieved success in working with the Juvenile Detention Home and Judge Benjamin Lindsey's juvenile court. The establishment of a Children's Bureau and codification of children's laws at the state and federal levels can be attributed to the work of the clubwomen.

These philanthropic activities continued after 1914, but with Denver and the nation immersed in a world war and the depression of the 1930s, these projects took a back seat to war service and emergency aid to the needy. In Denver, six clubs known for their earlier philanthropic activities took the lead in this new work. The members of the Fortnightly, Monday Literary, Twenty-Second Avenue Study, Round Table, Woman's, and North Side clubs plunged into war work, along with clubwomen across the nation. In Denver, this meant belonging to the Red Cross, the Liberty Bond drives, the Council of Defense, and various other committees and agencies organized at the time. Individually and collectively, Denver clubwomen were a major reason why Denver was called "one big United Service Organization center."[14]

This study does not attempt to cover the activities of all clubs in Denver which were members of the state and national federations but merely to provide an analysis of six of the earliest, and most enduring, clubs. Other criteria for study were that the clubs originated between 1880 and 1900; that each was either a literary study group or a departmental club; and that each was in existence through the 1970s. Of the six selected, five—the Fortnightly, Monday Literary, Round Table, Twenty-Second Avenue Study, and Woman's clubs—were charter members of the Colorado Federation; the sixth, the North Side Woman's Club, was not a charter member but did join the state and national federations in 1895. As some of Denver's oldest clubs, these six provided much of the leadership, direction, and energy for the club work of the period and initiated many of the reforms and services rendered in Denver. It is hoped that this study will broaden the current knowledge of Colorado women reformers and the work of the clubwomen during this volatile period as well as show that community involvement and reform did not end with the Progressive era for the clubwomen of Colorado.

THE EARLY YEARS, 1881-1900

B Y THE 1880s Denver was an established western city. Within two decades, it had been transformed from a collection of makeshift shacks into the hub of a rapidly growing region. Two major causes of this growth, beginning in the early 1870s, were the booster efforts of Denver's leaders and the coming of the railroads. Community leaders like William Byers, Fred Z. Salomon, John Evans, Charles and Luther Kountze, and David H. Moffat had consistently publicized the virtues and advantages of the city and the Colorado region. At their urging, in 1872 the state legislature created and funded the Board of Immigration, whose job it was to encourage migration to Colorado.[1] In addition, Evans, Moffat, Luther Kountze, and Bela Hughes were instrumental in building the first railroad from Denver to Cheyenne to connect with the transcontinental line. Following that success, other rail lines were built into and out of Denver until by 1890 there were 4,176 miles of track in the state.[2]

Intent on profit and growth, however, Denver's power elite did little to ease the burdens of those whom they had encouraged to immigrate. As early as 1860, Byers, who was editor of the *Rocky Mountain News* and one of the city's chief boosters, persuaded the city government to raise a stipend for the poor, and by 1862 the county levied a tax for relief—but it was never enough. City and county authorities tried to push the burden off on each other, and many property owners felt that the indigents were unworthy of any aid.[3] But one of Denver's important early leaders, largely unrecognized, felt differently. In 1860 Elizabeth Byers, the wife of William Byers, organized the first charity devoted solely for relief of the poor. The Ladies Union Aid Society (later the Ladies Relief Society) healed the sick, tried to help deserted children find homes, and solicited contributions for food, clothing, and money. Ultimately it established a kindergarten, a day nursery, a free clinic, a home for destitute women and children, and a home for the aged.[4]

The divergence of interests that characterized male and female attitudes toward social problems in Denver also divided the social worlds of men and women. While the city's male leaders established private clubs in which to socialize and discuss business, their wives—many of whom were involved in the Ladies Relief Society or church organizations—felt the need to broaden their knowledge and horizons. Both were similar, however, in that they took their cues from the East.

Denver Fortnightly Club   On April 13, 1881, eleven women met at the home of Ella S. Denison to organize a women's literary club on the model of the Fortnightly Club of Chicago, to which Denison's mother had belonged. The first minutes describe the purpose of the club as "a union of congenial minds for study and discussion and for the furtherance of good in practical ways."[5]   Between 1881 and 1900, the Denver Fortnightly Club met on the second and fourth Wednesdays of each month from October through April, presenting a yearly total of twelve papers on any subject. Following a member's reading of her paper, open discussion ensued—but without unkind criticism, for, as one member put it, "This *seems* to prove that *intelligent* study makes one tollerant [*sic*] of another's views, even when not agreeing with them."[6]   Topics given during the first two decades of this club included "Woman's Influence through Literature," "A Plea for Some Neglected Points in the Education of Women," "French Art," and "Industrial Education."   The women combined topics of general interest and of the classics in art and literature with relevant issues of the day.   In particular, Denison's 1896 paper, "How Can the Labor Problem Be Solved?" discussed conciliation and arbitration, profit-sharing, and cooperation as solutions to this thorny problem of the 1890s.[7]

Of the original twelve women who founded the Fortnightly Club, all were married to, or widows of, businessmen, physicians, educators, public servants, or religious leaders.[8]   (See appendix for names of charter members in all clubs under discussion.)   The women themselves, according to available records, did not work outside the home.   However, some of them, like Ella Denison, Margaret Gray Evans, and Ione Hanna, had long histories of involvement in city affairs.   Ella Denison was a director of the Denver Orphans' Home, a founder of the Denver YMCA in 1887, an organizer of the Civil Service Reform League and City Improvement Society, and president of the Old Ladies' Home in 1900. Margaret Gray Evans, the second wife of Governor John Evans, was a member of the Ladies Union Aid Society, an organizer of the Ladies Relief Society in 1874, and president of the Denver Orphans' Home. Ione Hanna, an avid suffragist, was the state suffrage organizer and led the successful fight for Colorado's equal suffrage amendment in 1893.

Over the years, the Denver Fortnightly Club remained small—by 1916 it counted only seventy members, past and present—but it was stable and enduring.[9] Club records, however, reveal that a significant number of members failed to attend and participate in meetings. By the end of the century, a group of newer members set out to revive the club, among them Anna Wolcott, a graduate of Wellesley College who became the principal of Wolfe Hall in Denver (1892–98).[10] In 1898, the same year that she joined the Fortnightly Club, she founded the Wolcott School as a young women's "high-class college preparatory school" with courses in English, mathematics, history, science, foreign languages, art, and literature. In many respects, the school reflected Wolcott's urbane interests and reformist views. Not only did the students receive a quality academic education, but they were also exposed to social issues of the day: The school program for 1909–10, for example, included a guest lecture by Jane Addams of Chicago's Hull House on the relation of playgrounds to child labor.[11] Graduates of the Wolcott School included the daughters of Denver's elite, many of whom would later join the city's white women's clubs as their mothers had done.

Monday Literary Club   Like the Denver Fortnightly Club, the Pleasant Hours Club was organized in 1881—to be renamed the Monday Literary Club eight years later. Founded by Ermina D. Ferris, it met every Monday, and its members studied and discussed the works of well-known authors on various subjects.[12] After joining the Colorado Federation of Women's Clubs as a charter member, the Literary Club grouped its studies into art, philosophy, education, literature, and science. In the 1890s, however, Americans became concerned about imperial expansion, business consolidations, and municipal government. Thus, while their husbands discussed these issues in board meetings and at the Denver Club, the clubwomen gave papers on protection and free trade, industrial problems, socialism, trends in education, and municipal reform. Contrary to many clubs, in 1897 the Literary Club discussed suffrage at one of its meetings, but it is worth noting that this was three years *after* Colorado women had received the right to vote.[13]

The composition of the Monday Literary Club was similar to that of the Fortnightly Club. Of the twenty-three members listed in the 1893–94 yearbook (the earliest extant), seventeen were married to businessmen and three others, respectively, to a lawyer, a teacher, and a physician. One of the women, Mary Barker Bates, was herself a physician, and the lone single woman, Ada Bingham, listed no occupation. While the Literary Club remained at or near its membership limit of twenty-five (and then thirty) from the 1880s through World War I, it suffered as many attendance problems as had the Fortnightly Club. Between 1881 and 1889 the average attendance remained at twelve, dropping occasionally to as low as five, and rose slightly to sixteen during the 1890s. Reasons given in the minutes were sickness, bad weather, and travel, but the frequency of the club's meetings—weekly rather than once or twice a month, as practiced by other clubs—may have been a more influential factor.[14]

Nevertheless, by 1918 one third of the current members of the Literary Club had belonged for over twenty years and two thirds for over eleven, demonstrating their loyalty and dedication. Although a few may be considered "working women," the majority were married, did not work outside the home, belonged to two or more clubs, and were involved in philanthropic work. Among these were Dr. Mary Barker Bates,[15] who helped to establish one of the first medical dispensaries in Denver and was a staff member of the Florence Crittenton Home for unwed mothers, the Cottage Home, and Woman's Hospital; Nettie E. Caspar,[16] an artist, a board member of the YWCA, a member of the Archaeological Institute, and past president of the State Board of Charities and Corrections; Mary E. Dunklee,[17] a poet and teacher; Helen Marsh Wixson,[18] an established magazine and newspaper writer who became state superintendent of public instruction; and Helen Ring Robinson,[19] a suffragist who in 1912 became the first woman elected to the Colorado state legislature.

Other well-known members were Sara Taylor Arneill,[20] Eva LeFevre,[21] Phoebe McAllister,[22] Virginia Morrison Shafroth,[23] Margaret Patterson Campbell,[24] and Elisabeth Spalding.[25]

Round Table Club   The third club, the Round Table Club, began in 1889 with twenty-five charter members. Founded, led, and dominated for thirty-two years by Alice Polk Hill, Colorado's first poet laureate, the club concentrated on presenting and discussing three papers at each Friday meeting.[26] Although the Round Table Club joined the General Federation in 1893 and the Colorado Federation as a charter member in 1895, its early literary beginnings always dominated its interests.

As with the other two clubs, the Round Table Club consisted primarily of the wives of businessmen.[27] As time went on, however, this constituency changed to include more women whose husbands represented the professions, especially law, and those whose husbands, whether in law or business, were more prominent than in the club's earlier years. By 1918, for instance, the Round Table Club's membership included Julie R. Bennett, wife of Horace W. Bennett, Cripple Creek developer; Virginia Morrison Shafroth, wife of Colorado politician John Shafroth; and the wives of Clayton C. Dorsey of the Hughes and Dorsey law firm and of John L. Stearns, president of the German-American Life Insurance Company.[28]

Perhaps it was the magnetism of Alice Hill's personality or the variety of papers presented each meeting that kept attendance high at the Round Table Club. Minutes from 1891 to 1921 show an average of twenty-one—approximately 70 percent of the active members compared to 33 and 40 percent, respectively, for the Denver Fortnightly and Monday Literary clubs.[29] Whatever the reason, such dedication and interest cannot be explained by the infusion of new blood alone, because after three decades over half of the club's members had belonged for over twenty years.

Twenty-Second Avenue Study Club   The Twenty-Second Avenue Study Club, unlike the earlier organizations, was not founded as a literary club but as an instrument of the suffrage movement. Originally called the Twenty-Second Avenue Non-

Partisan Equal Suffrage League, it was organized in October 1893 as an auxiliary to the Colorado Equal Suffrage Association, which was founded in 1870 after Elizabeth Cady Stanton and Susan B. Anthony visited Colorado at the request of Mary Thompson McCook, wife of Governor Edward McCook.[30] Louise Tyler, state organizer, and Ione T. Hanna (who also belonged to the Fortnightly Club) aided in the organization.

The work of the Twenty-Second Avenue Non-Partisan Equal Suffrage League and other state suffrage organizations proved eventually successful, for Colorado's woman suffrage amendment passed on November 7, 1893. Ten days later the club, looking for a reason for its further continuance, voted to study Fiske's *Civil Government of the United States*, to report on the leading political questions of the day, and to study Shattuck's *Parliamentary Rules*. In March and April of 1894, its members attended a series of lectures on civil government under the auspices of the Colorado Equal Suffrage Association. During the summer and fall, they devoted their time to activities related to the November elections—among them the election of club member Ione Hanna to the school board.[31]

After winning suffrage for Colorado women, the members of the Equal Suffrage League voted to dissolve the organization at a meeting on December 28, 1894, and to form, in its place, the Twenty-Second Avenue Study Club. Twenty-four of those present clearly had no interest in participating further, but the remaining nineteen continued pursuing their interest in political questions, beginning with a study of Hatch's *Constitution and Civil Government of Colorado* and of current events.[32] During the club's first five years, four charter members resigned and were replaced by nine new members to bring the total club membership to twenty-five, its limit for several years.[33]

In 1898 the club's constituency included the wives of businessmen, lawyers, and one pastor—an occupational characterization that changed little over the years. Like the other clubs, very few of its members were single, and its two single members in 1898 are not listed in the Denver City Directory as having occupations outside the home.[34] The most stable of the clubs under consideration, the Twenty-Second Avenue Club had a waiting list for much of its early history.[35] For over five years no members left the club voluntarily; then, beginning in 1903, five of the original members resigned over the next five years. After 1907, only death removed any of the original members from the rolls. Such dedication meant that most of these women could claim *decades* of membership.

While no mention is made in club records of the degree to which members participated, a number were regularly officers or board members, indicating high involvement. Nettie E. Caspar was founder and president from 1893 to 1924, at which time declining health forced her to step down. Maude Weisser, another charter member, was then elected acting president, but the women's loyalty to Caspar led them to retain her as their honorary president. Her death in 1932 occasioned heartfelt grief and a sense of loss in the five surviving charter members, the newer members of the club, and among Denver clubwomen at large.

Woman's Club of Denver By 1894 Colorado clubwomen showed considerable interest in forming a large departmental club (one that was subdivided into issue-based departments such as reform, philanthropy, and art and literature) similar to those found in eastern cities. Ella Denison, the founder of the Fortnightly Club, led the drive, along with twelve other members of this and the Literary and Roundtable clubs. In March they announced a public meeting to organize the Woman's Club of Denver. Two hundred clubwomen—suffragists, reformers, and working women—met in April 1894 to organize the new club.[36] Sarah Platt Decker, its first president, presided over the early meetings, which were held at the YMCA on Champa and Eighteenth streets. Divided into the departments of home, education, philanthropy, art and literature, reform, and science and philosophy, the club's membership increased rapidly, reaching 1,000 members within a decade.[37] When the four older clubs met to issue the call for a state federation of women's clubs, they included the Woman's Club because it was Denver's largest. (Unlike most literary clubs, departmental clubs did not limit their membership.) Since it was a departmental club, the Woman's Club concentrated on reform and philanthropic work, although its members also pursued literary studies. In fact, for several years most of its members were in the department of art and literature, and every one of the club's departments generated papers or invited speakers and lecturers to its meetings.

Under the leadership of Sarah Platt Decker, a woman of immense personal magnetism and energy, the Woman's Club grew rapidly in its early years.[38] Although Decker took a vigorous part in the 1893 suffrage campaign, she achieved her reputation in the women's club movement. As the first president of the Woman's Club, she directed its social welfare work, and she so impressed delegates at the biennial convention of the General Federation of Women's Clubs, held in Denver in 1896, that she was elected federation vice president two years later. She refused the presidential nomination in 1902 but accepted it in 1904 and served two terms (1904–8). Her wit and good judgment remained memorable qualities of her leadership: "Her addresses to the federation," states Edward T. James in *Notable American Women*, "reveal a keen sense of the practical, an ability to cut to the core of a problem and devise workable solutions. Illustrative of her incisiveness was her terse reply to the president of a New York musical club who had complained that its members were bored with singing to themselves: 'Try to sing to others. My busy day. Excuse brevity.'"[39]

Decker's talents brought her recognition and honors outside the sphere of club work as well. In 1908 she was the only woman among the national leaders invited to President Theodore Roosevelt's conference on the conservation of natural resources. In Colorado, she was a member of the Board of Charities and Corrections (1898–1912), the state civil service commission, the Denver Civic Federation, and the Woman's Public Service League. On her sudden death in 1912, flags in Denver were flown at half-mast, and a memorial held in her honor drew representatives from many women's groups, including the Equal Suffrage Association, the Women's Christian Temperance Union, the Women's Relief Corps, the Colorado Federation of Women's Clubs, and, of course, the Woman's Club of Denver.[40]

North Side Woman's Club   The last of the six clubs, the North Side Woman's Club, benefited from the popularity and success of its predecessors. One hundred sixty-six women signed the charter roll in 1895 and elected Sarah A. Wolff, its originator, as founder and temporary chair. Meeting at the home of Frances M. Wheeler, its organizers drew up a constitution and elected Martha A. B. Conine as president and Sarah Wolff as first vice president. The group selected Arbuckle Hall as the club's meeting place and established departments along the lines of the General and Colorado federations: home and education, literature and science, and reform and philanthropy.[41] In the following year, the club added a department of social affairs.

Although not a charter member of the Colorado Federation, the North Side Club joined as soon as possible and thereafter faithfully followed the federation's guidelines. Between 1895 and 1900, the department of home and education, under the guidance of Sarah Irish, Millie Johnston, and Mary L. Parks, reflected some of the issues of the period: scientific cooking, dietetics, practical education, manual training programs, and methods of discipline. It also addressed the issue of increasing opportunities for women in higher education with a paper in 1899 that asked the question, "Does Higher Education Make Our Girls Unfit for Wifehood and Motherhood?" Members of the literature and science department, led by Mary Chase, Harriet G. R. Wright, and Jeannette M. Starr, discussed American humorists, poetry, the Crusades, and regional American writers while also exploring advances in science, electricity, and aerial navigation.

Ironically, the department of reform and philanthropy, the North Side club's smallest, furnished many of the studies and initiated much of the work that would become its most important—from local charities and economic issues like the Single Tax and women as wage earners to political questions like the initiative and referendum, civil service, and prominent socialists.[42] These discussions naturally led to agitation, reform, and philanthropic work by women in this and other clubs. As Eleanor Flexner writes in *Century of Struggle*,

the club movement served as a kind of forcing area which propelled [women] into a world of enlarging horizons, new experiences, and new contacts. . . . To the extent that a woman moved into leadership posts and traveled to state or even national conventions, she came into contact with a powerful mix of ideas and activities.[43]

The experiences of the two departmental clubs, the Woman's Club of Denver and the North Side Woman's Club, differed from those of the smaller organizations. Having no membership limits, both were free to grow as much as possible—the Woman's Club to 920 members by the end of Sarah Decker's term in 1899, and the North Side Club to 150 (later stabilized at about 125).[44] But unlike the smaller clubs, turnover in both of these organizations was great. By 1918, fewer than 10 percent of the members in each club had belonged for over twenty years. In comparison, the rate of membership stability was 36 percent for the Denver Fortnightly Club, 30 percent for the Monday Literary Club, 60 percent for the Round Table Club, and 50 percent for the Twenty-Second Avenue Club.

In addition, while the majority of members in these two clubs were the wives of businessmen, lawyers, doctors, public servants, educators, and religious leaders, they also—especially the Woman's Club—had a large number of reformers, suffragists, public servants, and working women.[45] Among the two hundred charter members of the Woman's Club were also twenty-six working women, including several professionals. The Denver City Directory of 1894–95 lists eighty women physicians, two newspaper reporters, one writer, one lecturer, one milliner, three county clerks, two college professors, and eight public school teachers.[46] Thus, while most of Denver's white clubwomen were married, unemployed outside the home, and content to express their views largely through club papers and presentations, a few women in many of the clubs—but primarily the Woman's Club of Denver—went against the norm in either their economic independence or active leadership outside of the club world.

Whatever the role taken by clubwomen, they were bound by loyalty and dedication to their clubs and to each other.[47] When a member was forced to resign because of ill health or increased family obligations, her sister members often rejected the proffered resignation, or they would list her as an honorary member in the hope that she would eventually return to full participation; in other cases, resignations were accepted with deep regret. Members who moved away often kept in close touch with the club, and sometimes they continued to receive the benefits of membership, such as yearbooks and histories.[48] When a club member died, the others usually honored her with resolutions sent to her family—or, as in the case of Alice Polk Hill, resolutions might be sent from one club to another. "Our city has lost one of its representative and forward looking citizens," said the Monday Literary Club of Hill, a member of the Round Table Club. "All Clubwomen have lost one of the Pioneers in the club movement . . . and we who knew her lost a dear and valued friend and companion."[49]

The Denver Fortnightly Club chose to honor its deceased members with memorial books presented to the Denver Public Library, a special recipient of the club's charity. The requirements for a memorial book were that it be something that the library wanted, that it be beautiful, and that it be on a subject of interest to the deceased. In memory of Elisabeth Spalding the gift was a book of her watercolors, while for Mrs. William Spalding it was the "Overland Diary of James A. Pritchard" edited by Dale Morgan.[50]

Within the club community, social interaction took place on several levels—individually, among club members, and between clubs. Many women often attended the same churches and socialized with other women through their husbands and children. Some women, especially those who were leaders of reform and philanthropic work, were members of more than one club. And clubs themselves held yearly guest days to which members of other clubs were invited, or they held joint meetings when a prominent speaker was in town. The Woman's Club of Denver, which had its own large clubhouse, was often the site for such interclub gatherings.

FROM THE START of the club movement, Denver clubwomen widened the sphere of women's involvement in social, political, and economic issues. Strangely enough, they met with little resistance at first—due largely, perhaps, to their stated intention of organizing primarily for *literary* study and because they were hardly rabble-rousers or vocal critics of the status quo. As has been mentioned, they gave their clubs innocuous names and prohibited discussion of controversial topics such as religion and woman suffrage—at least until suffrage had become a fact in Colorado.[51] Thus, to all outward appearances, the clubs were "universities for middle-aged women."

Furthermore, clubwomen thoroughly studied social problems and their solutions firsthand before offering their ideas to the community at large. With great political wisdom, they invited prominent men—leaders in government, education, and religion—to lecture at their meetings. Some of these guest speakers included the Reverend Thomas Uzzell and William Jennings Bryan, both of whom were guests at the Woman's Club of Denver; Judge Benjamin Barr Lindsey, who spoke on juvenile delinquency at the North Side Women's Club; and Mayor Robert Speer and Governor George Carlson, who addressed the latter club in 1915.[52] The men were often won over by the women's sincerity, knowledge, and well-placed praise. So impressed were they with Susan Ashley's political acumen that state legislators held a special evening session to hear her speak on the need for a state home for dependent children, after which the body voted in favor of such an institution.[53] In other respects, too, women enlisted the support of leading progressive men—John Shafroth, Ben Lindsey, George Creel, and Thomas Patterson, all of whom were supporters and co-reformers. Patterson, in particular, allowed the Woman's Club of Denver to publish the 1894 Christmas edition of his newspaper, the *Rocky Mountain News,* and to keep the profits from this issue, which emphasized the Colorado suffrage campaigns of 1878 and 1893 and the current work of Denver's women's clubs.[54]

A third reason for the women's early success in gaining the support of public opinion was their choice of causes—the rights of children, the aged, women, and the disadvantaged. Not until later did they turn their attention to criticism of monopolies and boss politics. Yet no matter how slowly, meticulously, and tactfully they pressed for reform, eventually they met with resistance and, in some cases, hostility. On the national level, former president Grover Cleveland in 1905 criticized the suffrage movement and the federated women's clubs in an article

for the *Ladies Home Journal.* "To those of us," he stated, "who
. . . cling to our faith in the saving grace of simple and unadul-
terated womanhood, any discontent on the part of woman with
her ordained lot, or a restless desire on her part to be and to do
something not within the sphere of her appointed ministrations,
cannot appear otherwise than as perversions of a gift of God to
the human race."[55] Cleveland insisted that the General Federation of Women's Clubs would mar home life, the community,
and the nation as women got into the "club habit." He wrote
that "the best and safest club for a woman to patronize was her
home" and that the suffrage movement would undermine the
character of wives and mothers.[56] Nor was President Cleveland
the only critic of women's clubs. Closer to home, Henry Buchtel, former governor of the state and chancellor of the University of Denver, stated that only the "dregs of womanhood"
voted in Colorado and that mothers had to be driven to the
polls to vote. In response, Adelle Bailey, president of the
Woman's Club of Denver, and Governor John Shafroth asserted
that women voters had a positive effect on Colorado.[57]

While the women's club movement met resistance both
locally and nationally, especially when it was allied with the
suffrage movement, Denver's clubwomen forged ahead with
social welfare projects that resulted in little ideological skir-
mishing. With their origins in literary study, the clubs recognized the city's need for a public library. In January 1885 three
members of the Denver Fortnightly Club joined a seven-mem-
ber committee to form the City Library Association; from this
early involvement, following the establishment of the Denver
Public Library in 1889, emerged the club's tradition of presenting the library with a memorial book honoring deceased members.[58] The Woman's Club of Denver, recognizing the broader
need to bring books into communities statewide, formed the
Traveling Library project in 1896, a philanthropic effort that was
eventually assumed by the Colorado Federation and placed under
the direction of Minnie J. Reynolds and Julia V. Welles, who
became nationally known for her work on this project. All of
the clubs soon joined in this work, usually donating boxes of
books in honor of a past president. By 1903, when the state
legislature authorized Free Traveling Libraries with a $1,000

appropriation, books were being sent to some sixty rural schools.[59]

Other early projects of Denver's clubwomen addressed problems of the needy, unemployed, homeless, and untrained. Both the Woman's Club of Denver and the North Side Women's Club began Pingree Gardens in the 1890s, an agricultural experiment designed to feed the poor while eliminating unsightly weed-covered vacant lots.[60] Clubs also pushed for the establishment of the State Home for Dependent Children, which opened in 1895, and the State Industrial School for Girls, which was established five years later. Once founded, their boards of control were dominated by Denver clubwomen like Jane O. Cooper, who was the first president of the industrial school, and Dora Reynolds, who sat on the board of the state home from its inception until her death in 1916. Other institutions which drew attention were the Newsboys' Union, the county hospital, the city jail, the Florence Crittenton Home for unwed mothers, and the Old Ladies Home, which developed from the Ladies Aid Society.[61]

Finally, Denver clubwomen supported two projects that typified the emerging Progressive spirit of the late nineteenth century—one a school of domestic science and the other a major landmark in cultural preservation. First, members of the Woman's Club of Denver, after studying methods of teaching kitchen-gardening (or scientific housekeeping) and cooking, organized the School of Domestic Science under the leadership of Annie G. Whitmore. Club members taught classes in cooking and kitchen-gardening to mostly poor young women in the Delgany and Colfax districts, the People's Tabernacle, Haymarket Haven, and Cathedral Missions. The project became so popular that the school became independent of the club and established an employment bureau for its graduates.[62] Second, in 1894 the Monday Literary and the Denver Fortnightly clubs jointly signed a petition brought to Denver by Virginia McClurg, a pioneer preservationist whose campaign to protect prehistoric ruins in southwest Colorado led in 1906 to the establishment of Mesa Verde National Park. In the intervening years—at least until McClurg formed her own Cliff Dwellings Association in 1900—the Colorado Federation, as well as the General Federation, lobbied vigorously for the cause.[63]

THE PROGRESSIVE YEARS, 1900-1914

THE ARRIVAL of the new century generated enthusiasm and hope for solutions to many troubling problems. In the United States this period, from 1900 to 1914, is commonly referred to as the Progressive era. It was a time when men and women began working vigorously for change. They sought to wrench government from the clutches of big business and place it once again in the hands of the people. They favored social reforms that would make life better for city dwellers, and they supported improved conditions for workers, especially women and children. Abuses by big business and municipal governments were graphically portrayed by the Muckrakers: Ida Tarbell's *History of the Standard Oil Company*, Lincoln Steffens's *The Shame of the Cities*, and Upton Sinclair's *The Jungle* exposed varying abuses in American society. Awakened by these books, by articles in magazines and newspapers, and by their own work with the city poor and disadvantaged, the Progressives worked for change at all levels of government. Their chief champion at the national level was Theodore Roosevelt, president from 1901 to 1909, whose years in office brought a number of reforms, including conservation of natural resources and legislation providing for meat inspection and pure food and drugs.

In Denver and Colorado, the Progressive movement brought together professionals in law, education, medicine, and business with members of municipal agencies, civic organizations, and, of course, women's clubs. At the state level, John Shafroth and Edward Costigan became well known for their reform work, and at the city level Judge Benjamin Lindsey began the juvenile court, Emily Griffith founded the innovative Opportunity School, and Robert Speer transformed Denver through his City Beautiful programs. In addition, Josephine Roche, police matron, and George Creel, "a voice of the people," made their impact on the city during this time.[1] Together, working at various levels, Denver Progressives were able to accomplish much in the way of positive change for the city, state, and nation. And for the first time in American history, women played a key role.

While embarking on works of reform and philanthropy, clubwomen continued to combine literary study of the classics with research and discussion of important social, political, and economic issues. In fact, their continuing interest in social issues prepared them individually for increasing roles outside the home and family. In Denver some clubs used yearly themes to guide the education of their members, while others, like the Denver Fortnightly Club, invited papers on any subject. These ranged from biographical studies of Henrik Ibsen and Jane Addams to issues like child labor, woman suffrage, and nature preservation.[2]

In the Monday Literary Club, current events in literature, domestic and foreign policy, education, and the social sciences took precedence during the presidency of Ada Bingham (1899–1900). Addressing the Russian-Japanese War, Caroline Walker's presentation took "the club on a political tour around the world, giving the most important events of the summer, and up to the present time when Russia and Japan are showing their teeth at each other in a most threatening manner."[3] In later years the club discussed "The New Educational Problems" and "Modern Wizards of Science." The Round Table Club, meanwhile, spent the Progressive years engrossed in the study of other countries. Always ambitious in their academic pursuits, club members studied United States history from "early explorations" to "present day problems" during 1912–13—an average of three to five papers each meeting.[4] Finally, the Twenty-Second Avenue Study Club alternated "theme" years with "miscellaneous" programs. Yearly themes of the period included "Africa," "The Victorian Age of Literature," "England," "India," and, in 1909–10, "United States and Possessions" with a stereoptican lecture on Alaska. Included among the miscellaneous programs were an illustrated talk about book plates by Chalmers Hadley and a talk by the Boy Scout commissioner.[5]

As departmental clubs, the Woman's Club of Denver and the North Side Woman's Club divided their studies into topics decided upon by the departments. At times these clubs relied on the services of the Reciprocity Bureau, a subcommittee of the Colorado Federation that received papers from members of the federated clubs and offered them to other clubs for presentation. However, that idea was greeted in the Fortnightly Club with such "horror and withering scorn that no one dared mention this possible source again."[6] The Fortnightly Club remained convinced that using another's paper was "cheating" and missed the intent of the process, which was to develop a woman's reading, writing, and analyzing skills.

Following the Spanish-American War and the nation's acquisition of Pacific territories, the home and education department of the Woman's Club of Denver appropriately discussed "Our New Possessions: The Philippines, Hawaii, Puerto Rico, and Samoa" at one of its meetings, and the department of social science held meetings relevant to current social problems and proposals such as the economic condition of women, racial programming, and Japanese immigration. All of these topics struck responsive chords for women who were leaving the home for outside employment, where eugenics was a new "scientific" theory that many people embraced, and where the restriction of Japanese immigration to the United States was disrupting relations between the two countries.[7]

Because the vast majority of clubwomen had children, they belonged to the vanguard of reform in education. Some of these women had also been teachers before getting married—at which point school policies, household duties, and societal expectations forced most to quit the profession. In the North Side Club's department of home and education, discussion on education reflected personal concerns as well as the progress of education in the United States. One 1901 paper asked "Is Anything Better than the United States School System?" Another, in 1903, asked "Is Home Leaving Too Much to the Schools?"—a question that is still being debated in the late twentieth century. The movement for vocational and physical education also received attention, with topics addressing the role of trade schools—particularly Denver's Manual Training High School—and physical education.

Prior to its reorganization as the department of social science, the North Side Club's department of reform and philanthropy combined studies of social work ("Social Settlements" and "City Missions"), state institutions ("Do State Reformatories Reform?" and "Asylums for the Feebleminded"), and political issues ("Municipal Reforms" and "The Condition of Local Government"). Meanwhile, the art and literature department focused on less debatable topics, exploring the works of Edgar Allen Poe, Oliver Wendell Holmes, and William Cullen Bryant, along with book reviews and travelogs.

Whatever the programs chosen and the topics selected, the process itself—reading, researching, writing, speaking, and discussing—increased the self-confidence, knowledge, and skills of many clubwomen. They became aware of their own abilities and of the social issues of their community. In short, Denver clubwomen—awakened to social problems as never before, fortified by their networks within the club world, backed by the resources of the General and Colorado federations, and led by some of the city's most experienced reformers, suffragists, philanthropists, and professional working women—embarked on a twenty-year campaign of reform.[9]

Much of the reform and philanthropic work of the Denver clubs during the Progressive era can be divided into four areas: libraries and education, health and welfare, youth, and conservation. The Traveling Library, which continued to receive help from the Colorado Federation, was unique to Colorado among the nation's federated clubs. For this reason, in 1902 the Colorado Federation was asked to submit one of its boxes of books to the St. Louis Exposition as an example of the contributions of American clubwomen to their communities and state. The following year, a five-member Library Commission (three of whom were clubwomen) was established in the state to handle the Traveling Library project. In 1906 the Twenty-Second Avenue Club honored its long-term president, Nettie Caspar, with a donation of books in her name, and sent another box in 1910 to honor deceased club members. The North Side Club, being larger, was able to send a box every other year during the Progressive period—a project that flourished until its chief promoter and director, Julia V. Welles, died in 1912. When the state legislature failed to appropriate sufficient funds for the Traveling Library Commission in 1913, the Twenty-Second Avenue Club joined with another, the Reviewers' Club, to petition the governor for immediate relief.[10] These two clubs received additional help from the others, and by 1918 the Traveling Library consisted of over 300 trunks containing over 9,000 books.[11]

Clubwomen fought for improved education on all fronts. During the administration of Colorado Federation president Minnie L. Harding, a scholarship and loan fund was established for girls and young women in Colorado who could not otherwise get an education. Later named in honor of its originator, the scholarship fund was a favorite of the member clubs. The first subscriptions came from a Canon City banker (Harding's home club was the Friends in Council Club in Canon City), Sarah Platt Decker, and Harding herself. One of the fund's success stories, according to Neata M. Preiss in a 1970 history of the Colorado Federation, was Edna V. Fisher of Pueblo, who "graduated with honors from the State Normal School at Greeley in 1903. She then taught in the Public Schools of Pueblo. Later she graduated from Teachers College of Columbia University in New York City and taught in Carnegie Technical School in Pittsburgh, Pennsylvania."[13]

The legislative committees in each of the clubs, as well as in the Colorado Federation, urged the passage of bills and resolutions designed to enhance educational opportunities, to provide for special educational programs, and to better provide for the teachers of the state. In this vein, the clubs advocated many new ideas in education: consolidated schools, teacherages for teacher residences in rural districts, manual training programs, art and music education, and domestic science classes. Legislative bills endorsed by the clubs included a public school teachers' pension bill, increased salaries for teachers, a measure for the establishment of manual training and a trade school, and a bill for the inspection of school buildings.[14]

Realizing that their voices would be more readily heard if they were members of the educational community, clubwomen also ran for school boards and pushed for the appointment of their sister clubwomen to university boards and state educational agencies. A number of women, beginning with Ione Hanna of the Denver Fortnightly Club, were elected to the school boards. Anne Shuler was the first dean of women at the University of Denver, and Anna Wolcott Vaile, who had taught at Wolfe Hall and had founded Miss Wolcott's School in 1898, was appointed the first woman regent for the state university. All of these women were members of the Fortnightly Club.[15]

In addition to advocating certain educational reforms and endorsing legislative bills, the clubwomen did the small things that endeared them to the educational communities. During the club year 1912–13, the North Side Club entertained the women teachers of their district, and in 1902–3 it held a school picnic which netted $300 for beautifying the walls of the school buildings. That same year, the women placed architectural photos in the halls of the high school.[16]

An even more extensive list of achievement can be found in programs that clubwomen initiated for health and welfare—in particular, the Old Ladies' Home, a free employment bureau, free dispensary, and day nursery. Several clubs maintained rooms at the Old Ladies' Home, periodically refurnishing them and providing aid and entertainment to the residents, especially around the holidays.[17] The city of Denver later took over the employment bureau, and the city hospital grew out of the free dispensary of the Woman's Club of Denver.[18] The day nursery for the children of working women, long a project of its founder, the Woman's Club, is now the Marjory Reed Mayo Nursery, named after its later benefactor.[19] Finally, legislation sponsored or supported by the clubs included equal guardianship of children, the State Employment Bureau (which became a reality in 1910), the State Board of Charities and Corrections, the Mothers' Compensation Act, and the Child Labor Act, passed in 1912.

While most of the clubs supported the same projects and legislative bills, the Denver Fortnightly Club was much more independent-minded. Although it joined with the others to support the Traveling Library appropriation bill, the teachers' pension, the establishment of a Children's Bureau, and the establishment of a state home for dependent children, it did not extend this support to the Consumers' League, the Prisoner's Aid Society, the Women's Auxiliary to the Juvenile Court, and the pure food bill of the Colorado state legislature. Although concerned with the plight of the poor, the children, and the women of the state, the club would not fund the Florence Crittenton Home, the Visiting Nurse Association, or the Salvation Army. Nor did the Day Nursery, the State Home for Mental

Defectives, or the Federal Employment Bureau of Women receive club monies. Perhaps one reason for its rejection of these projects is given by the daughter of one of its charter members, who said that they "were too close to their own homes to consider the problem of women playing any other role such as job holders, career women, or those in the business world."[20]

It also appears that the women of the Fortnightly, unlike others, did their philanthropic work *outside* of the club and not as part of their club membership. Stated club historian Harriet Campbell, the club "has no philanthropic committee because so many members are actively connected with philanthropic institutions on their own and the first objective has been the union of congenial minds for study and discussion."[21] Then, too, Fortnightly members also belonged to the Woman's Club of Denver and undoubtedly performed philanthropic work there.[22]

In reforms for youth, the women's clubs continued their support of the state homes for boys, girls, and dependent children. Through magazine subscriptions and income generated from entertainment, they contributed materially to maintenance of the homes while at the same time devoting their energies to these projects as members of the boards of control.[23] Clubwomen also endorsed the efforts of Judge Benjamin Lindsey and deferred to his judgment in regard to juveniles.[24] With the women's support, the Children's Bureau was established and child labor laws passed. Lindsey and George Creel wrote Ellis Meredith that "had it not been for the votes of women and their unceasing donations of time and money, few if any of our great welfare measures would have been enacted into law."[25]

Conservation, another important area of Progressive reform, was a favorite cause of clubwomen throughout Colorado. With an avid conservationist like Theodore Roosevelt in the White House, clubwomen finally succeeded in persuading Congress to set aside Mesa Verde and its cliff dwellings as a national park. As early as 1894 the Denver Fortnightly and Monday Literary clubs had signed petitions addressing this matter. Three years later, the Colorado Federation formed the Committee for the Preservation and Restoration of the Cliff and Pueblo Ruins of Colorado. For years, individual clubs held stereoptican lectures on the ruins, invited speakers to their meetings, and petitioned the state and national legislatures. The park, established in 1906, owed its creation to "the unrelenting pressure maintained by a group of some two hundred women for approximately a quarter of a century."[26] Other club-supported conservation measures were the establishment of the State Bureau of Forestry in 1909, one of whose members was Ella McNeil of the Fortnightly Club, and the National Park Service in 1916.[27]

Besides reform work coordinated through the Colorado and General federations, the Denver clubs also contributed to their own local projects. Women in the Fortnightly Club, for example, donated to the Endowment Fund for the Maria Mitchell Chair of Astronomy at Vassar College and the local YWCA Rest and Recreation Rooms. The Twenty-Second Avenue Club passed resolutions urging adoption of the Esch bill in 1912 to prohibit poisonous phosphorus in the manufacture of matches, endorsed the work of the Citizen's Protective League in 1913, and supported resolutions sent by the Woman's Public Service League in 1914 asking that two inspectors of public amusements be appointed by the Committee of Safety, one of which should be a woman.[29] The legislative committee of the Woman's Club of Denver helped to secure the passage of laws validating a married woman's will; providing for the examination of the eyes, ears, teeth, and lungs of schoolchildren; and appropriating money for a diphtheria antitoxin.[30] The second largest club, the North Side Woman's Club, sewed garments for the Social Union, gave towels to the Boys' Free Baths at the courthouse, established and supported the North Side Neighborhood House, and distributed gifts to needy children for Christmas.[31]

The early literary study conducted in the federated clubs from the 1880s to 1900 gave clubwomen valuable experience in research, writing, and public speaking. From this base of self-confidence and knowledge, and aided by the Colorado and General federations, they acquired additional skills in organization, lobbying, and mobilization. Through this pyramid structure—consisting of a national organization, state federations, and local clubs—clubwomen aroused, organized, and mobilized large numbers of their compatriots. Since clubwomen and their leaders were well known and well respected in their communities, Americans knew exactly where to turn in time of war.

THE WORLD WAR I YEARS, 1914-1919

D ENVER CLUBWOMEN, ever abreast of developments in the world, cast wary eyes across the ocean as the armies of Europe readied for war following the assassination of Archduke Francis Ferdinand in late June 1914. President Wilson had asked the American people to be neutral "in thought as well as in deed," yet other forces were stronger than the president's plea. Allied propaganda, close ties to their ancestral homes, and German submarine warfare against all seafaring vessels combined to bring Americans into this worldwide conflict on April 6, 1917. The clubwomen, who had already been busy preparing themselves for this day, were ready to answer the call to service.

From 1914 to 1919, the programs of the Denver clubs reflected the concerns and needs of the people and the nation. Prior to the nation's entry into the war, programs included "War Literature: Past and Present," the Bible, and "What Suffrage Has Done for Colorado." After April 1917, programs increasingly dealt with more serious problems and the changes brought on by the war: food conservation, medical preparedness, national defense, contributions of the Red Cross, and women in war work.[1] Often speakers were brought in to give their firsthand knowledge of the war efforts. Thomas Patterson, son and grandson of Fortnightly Club members, once spoke of his ambulance service work in France to the members of that club.[2]

By 1917 the nationwide fear of the German aggression, a public wariness of immigrants who had not become assimilated into American society, and the sensationalism of some of the nation's newspapers brought on renewed cries for Americanization.[3] Aliens living in Denver were herded off to internment camps in Utah while *The Denver Post* led a vicious attack on anything Teutonic. The names of every German alien woman residing in Denver, complete with home addresses, appeared in the paper, which also cautioned citizens to avoid buying soap, patent medicines, and food from unknown salespeople since these items might have been deliberately contaminated.[4] Although club records do not reveal an active role in this hysteria, the Fortnightly Club did agree to buy American products, on the urging of the committee of home economics, to combat German propaganda.[5] As patriotic members of the middle class, clubwomen joined the cries for Americanization and spent club meetings discussing the problems of immigration and assimilation.[6] But while these concerns of the clubwomen for immigrants and their different ways continued through the Red Scare, women continued to carry on the reform and philanthropic work begun in the Progressive years.

While war service work consumed much of the clubwomen's time and energy from 1914 to 1919, they did not neglect projects begun in earlier years—in particular, state institutions and commissions. Gertrude Vaille served as supervisor of relief on the Commission of Charities and Corrections, Anne Evans as City Library president of the Library Commission, Ellis Meredith as president of the election commission, and Mary C. C. Bradford as superintendent of public instruction.[7] During the war years, the clubs also continued to support the Crittenton Home, the Workshop for the Adult Blind, the two industrial schools, the YWCA Rest and Recreation Rooms, the Colorado Federation Scholarship Fund, and the Old Ladies' Home. In legislation, they helped secure a detention home for women, a child welfare bureau, a game refuge, and additional state monies for the Girls' Industrial School. Club-endorsed, but not passed by the legislature, were bills forbidding capital punishment, regulating child labor, providing for medical inspections in schools, and establishing a federal department of education.[8]

Colorado became a Prohibition state in 1916, four years before national Prohibition. Women in the state were instrumental in the passage of the dry law; however, very little mention can be found in club records themselves regarding Prohibition at the state or national level. Club historian Susan Riley Ashley noted in 1915 that the Fortnightly Club discussed the Prohibition act and that the members showed "remarkable insight into the far reaching implications, complications, and consequences" of the amendment, but does not elaborate on that discussion.[9]

In 1910 and 1911, the North Side Woman's Club voted to discuss temperance once each year, but no other local clubs showed any indication of their involvement with, or attitudes toward, Prohibition.[10] The Colorado Federation, under the administration of Nettie C. Jacobson, "emphasized cooperation with other organizations to make Colorado a Bone Dry state," yet a random survey of 127 members of the Denver clubs found only three who belonged to the Women's Christian Temperance Union (WCTU). Two of these women, Amy Cornwall and Mary L. Parks, were members of the North Side Woman's Club; the third, Antoinette Arnold Hawley, was a member of the Woman's Club of Denver.[12] It appears that the federated clubwomen kept an official "hands-off" policy regarding temperance until late in order to not jeopardize programs that they favored most.

The response to Prohibition by clubwomen was similar to their stance on the volatile issue of woman suffrage. Although individual members supported and worked for equal suffrage, the state and national federations did not endorse it until 1914.[13] Even Sarah Platt Decker, an ardent suffragist, kept suffrage off the federation's agenda, believing that the internal controversy would weaken without influencing the local clubs that disapproved of the vote—not to mention alarming the men.[14] One can safely assume that the clubwomen believed the idea of temperance to be a good one but that the political and legal problems that would ensue would make enforcement difficult. Thus, they avoided hurting their own programs by not publicly embracing a potentially damaging issue.

With the declaration of war in April 1917, munitions, medical supplies and services, money, and soldiers were desperately needed across the nation, and Colorado citizens responded enthusiastically. They registered for the draft, conserved food supplies, bought war savings stamps and Liberty Bonds, joined the Red Cross, and converted industrial plants to war production. For each of the two Red Cross membership drives, held in the spring of 1917 and 1918, Coloradans gave over $1 million, the ninth state per capita in the country.[15] They also supported Liberty Bond drives, the YWCA, Salvation Army, and the American Library Association ("For a million dollars for a million books for a million men").[16] But money was not the only object of their largess: Articles of clothing, medical supplies, entertainment, and food equally went to the Red Cross, the servicemen's centers, and the hospitals.

Having proved themselves to be capable of mobilizing large

numbers of women through the federated clubs, clubwomen were often appointed chairs of committees and committee members. The state chair of the women's Liberty Loan Committee, Helen Ring Robinson of the Woman's Club of Denver, traveled throughout the state urging women to support the war effort and the Liberty Loan drives. At the local level, the executive committee of the third Liberty Loan Drive, chaired by Round Table Club member Julie R. Bennett, included club members Marguerite Taussig and Mrs. William Berger. For that same drive, five of the nine members of the Ways and Means Committee were clubwomen.[17] The fourth and fifth Liberty Loan drives were so successful that they brought words of praise from Carter Glass, U. S. secretary of the treasury, who said: "The women of the United States have made an instant and magnificent response to every call which the government has made to them. Through the five Liberty Loans they have served with devotion, with zeal, and with self-sacrificing patriotism."[18]

The clubs bought as well as sold bonds. At an October 1917 meeting of the Fortnightly Club, Mary F. Fisher reported that $6,300 had been sold in the club's name.[19] In addition, in 1918 the club joined other women's clubs in providing entertainment at the Central Presbyterian Church, which raised $1,000 for the war funds.[20] The Round Table Club sent $50 from its treasury for a Liberty Bond,[21] and the Woman's Club, over the course of the war, purchased war bonds of $1,300 and sold $8,000 in bonds to its members.[22] To the North Side Women's Club went the honor of having been the first club to buy a bond from money set aside for the North Side Neighborhood House.[23]

As soon as the United States entered the war, Colorado governor Julius Gunter appointed men's and women's councils of defense, both of which consisted of prominent Coloradans. Nearly half of the women's council were clubwomen called "to assist and co-operate in solving all problems arising in the state during the preparations for war and after the struggle with Germany has actually begun."[24] Besides the Liberty Loan drives, these women traveled throughout the city appealing to the patriotism of citizens and calling for their support. Mass meetings for Denver clubwomen were held at the clubhouse of the Woman's Club, where in 1918 Beatrice Forbes-Robinson Hale, a representative of

Herbert Hoover's Food Administration Board, spoke to 500 women on the necessity of food conservation.[25] When queried by a news reporter, the "rich women of Denver" promised to do their part in this effort:

It is the only fair thing for those who can afford things, to adjust their living to set an example for all. Buying flour will make a proportionately greater hardship on those with small income[s] than with those who can afford luxury. Those who can should certainly ration themselves.[26]

As the war drew to a close, women who had been active in the home front effort envisioned the continuing involvement of women in the affairs of the state. Mrs. Kistler, chair of the Women's State Council of Defense, suggested the establishment of local bureaus for the placement of released army personnel, a listing of jobs so that women who were dropped from war work could find employment, and the continuation of thrift and economy—habits learned from the war. Realizing that demobilization and other social changes would increase the need for local charities, she advocated drafting experienced women into permanent social work.[27]

But the war was still being raged, and the demands on American productivity and relief were great. It was perhaps through their work for the Red Cross that the Denver women made their greatest impact. Each club regularly gave money to the Red Cross, beginning with the Belgian Flour Fund and the Belgian War Relief Fund and continuing throughout the war.[28] From the start, clubwomen joined the Denver chapter of the Red Cross. By 1916 the Red Cross "army" had collected two hundred volunteers for disaster or war relief. Since clothes, surgical dressings, and other medical supplies were priorities in Red Cross work, the women sewed, knitted, and rolled bandages during club meetings. "We dispensed with papers," said one, "and instead . . . worked at our knitting [while] one of our members read American history."[29]

The Red Cross also provided canteens and entertainment for the military personnel arriving to, stationed at, and departing from Denver. The largest canteen was at Union Station. The room—donated to the Red Cross by John Keating of the Denver Union Terminal Company and furnished by the terminal company, Daniels and Fisher, and the Denver Music Company—was open twenty-four hours a day. Here the "sammies" were given free cigarettes, candy, and stationery.[30] The Fortnightly Club's Elizabeth Keely, who ran this canteen, and Jennie Baker, a member of the Council of Defense, made the ultimate sacrifice: both died of exhaustion from their many hours of war service. Harriet Campbell, a sister clubwoman, later wrote of their dedication. Baker, she said,

> exhausted herself in her work, giving up nearly everything, even her own home. Returning one day, quite worn out, she stopped on her way to bed to write in the dust of her piano, "I am a patriot." Her duties as wife of the president of the State University for years may have prepared her mentally for public work, but it could not give her physical strength.

As for Elizabeth Keely,

> In her one to two daily trips to Fitzsimons Hospital[,] sick and dying soldiers were made more comfortable by assistance in their banking, wills, & letters. She found parched peas at a Greek food store for a Greek . . . She got up two hours earlier than everyone else for correspondence and household planning. The last day Mrs. Keely was able to be on her feet, was filled with usual duties. A few days later, she was not, for God took her.[31]

War service work also led to the death of Helen Ring Robinson. Serving as Colorado's first woman senator (1913–17) and chair of the state Women's Liberty Loan Committee (1917–19) weakened her health and she died in 1923.[32]

Elizabeth Keely and other Red Cross workers regularly visited and entertained the wounded at Fitzsimons Hospital. They donated food, postal cards, records, and flowers. In 1919 Lisbeth Fish, Elizabeth Keely, and six hundred women went to the hospital bearing gifts for the soldiers.[33]

While the Red Cross Motor Corps was generally made up of

young women, some of the officers were older clubwomen of Denver. Stated the *Rocky Mountain News* in 1918, "The motor branch reads like the social register of Denver but these society women, volunteering primarily because they are experienced at driving their own cars, mean business." The motor corps women took special courses in motor mechanics and auto repairing under Tom Botterill or at the YMCA motor school or in one of the two courses at the Opportunity School garage. The women were used for communication work when they were fully trained.[34]

The first service center for the military in Denver was the Soldiers' and Sailors' Club at 1436 Glenarm Place. The Woman's Club women gave the War Camp Community Service the use of their clubhouse at that address for the duration of the war. In the meantime, the women met at the Calvary Baptist Church. The club later received a citation from the federal government for its generosity.[35] The Denver clubs also contributed money to the furlough camps for American soldiers in France. Sponsored by the General Federation of Women's Clubs, these camps served as recuperation centers for American soldiers. The smaller clubs gave between $10 to $50, while the 356-member Woman's Club of Denver gave 100 percent of its quota, or $400.[36]

In addition to war work through the Women's Council of Defense, the YWCA, and the Red Cross, the clubwomen baked cookies, donated fruit and jelly, observed meatless and wheatless days, and contributed money and books for the Soldier Libraries.[37] Refreshments at meetings were often eliminated and programs for the war years were typed or handwritten and not bound as in previous years.

In all, the service record of the Denver federated clubs and their members was impressive. Because of their previous reform work, proven ability to mobilize and lead large numbers of women and to identify sources of money, and the respect accorded them by the citizens of Denver, the clubwomen were appointed chairs and committee members of state and local organizations devoted to the war effort. The faith in the women was well placed.

POSTWAR YEARS AND THE DEPRESSION, 1920-1940

FOR THE UNITED STATES and Colorado, the password of the 1920s was conformity. The Great Crusade of the First World War had only served to disillusion the patriots, the internationalists, and the progressives alike. The peace treaty at Versailles and the struggle for its ratification in the United States had reinforced the views of cynics and isolationists. War-induced nativism not only endured but worsened into the 1919–20 Red Scare. Seeing Communists everywhere and encouraged by the tactics of yellow journalism, politicians accused, arrested, and deported hundreds of suspected troublemakers. At the national level, Attorney General A. Mitchell Palmer led the way; in Denver, the *Post* incited such animosity from labor that its offices fell victim to rioting during the Denver Tramway strike of August 1920.[1] But having very little proof of any danger from Bolshevism, the scare dissipated by late 1920. This was not, however, the end of nativism or its silent partner, Americanism. Foreigners were still viewed with distrust, and anything or anyone not conforming was labeled un-American. Traditional minorities—Jews, African-Americans, and Catholics—found themselves targets of renewed intimidation and violence. The Ku Klux Klan experienced a revival, and in Colorado it captured important state offices.

For many of the women in the Denver clubs, the end of World War I meant a return to weekly or monthly literary study devoid of the clicking of Red Cross needles, to philanthropic work in the community, and to the endorsement of peace-keeping pacts. But the decade of the 1920s was not merely a return to the past; it was a breaking point. Club leaders of earlier years who had been the founders of local movement, who had stressed women's involvement in social welfare and legislative matters, and who had succeeded in pushing back the boundaries of woman's sphere—were reaching their seventies and eighties. Many of the prominent early leaders died in the 1920s, leaving the work to other women who had not been suffragists or reformers. While these new leaders in no way rolled back the advances of the previous forty years, they generally did not share the reformist zeal of their predecessors. Club work became quieter and less revolutionary; rather than leading new social reforms, the new clubwomen continued with the interests of the past and looked to the leadership of others.[2]

The signing of the armistice on November 11, 1918, marked the end of war service work and the beginning of Americanization efforts. As noted earlier, during the war the Denver clubs devoted great attention to immigration. So concerned were they over the implications of an unassimilated citizenry that the General and Colorado federations made Americanization their project from 1918 to 1920. In their effort to Americanize foreigners, clubwomen realized that they did not know the subject well enough to teach it; consequently, they turned to the study of government and citizenship.[3]

For many Coloradans immigration, crime, labor unrest, and political corruption led to an interest in a rapidly growing organization that promised to solve these social ills—the Ku Klux Klan. Founded in Colorado in 1921 under Dr. John Galen Locke, the state Grand Dragon, the Klan met no substantial counterattack in Denver and established a stronghold in the capital city. "The multifaceted image and platform of the Ku Klux Klan," states historian Robert Goldberg, "offered something for everyone"—for the anti-Jew, anti-Catholic, and anti-black; for the lodge men with its rituals and secrecy; and for the law and order advocates. By carefully juggling all these elements, Locke was able to achieve success.[4] Those who joined were generally white, male, native-born, Protestant, married, and middle-aged.[5]

In the 1923 election, Benjamin F. Stapleton, receiving Klan support, was elected mayor of Denver. In that same year, the Klan, with other strongholds in Pueblo, Canon City, and Grand Junction, elected prominent state officials sympathetic to its cause, including the governor, lieutenant governor, secretary of state, superintendent of public instruction, and a state supreme court justice. However, six representatives in the Klan-controlled house joined with the senate, led by Billy Adams, to prevent the passage of Klan bills.[6] By 1925 the combination of legislative inaction, corruption by Klansmen, and a federal charge of tax evasion against Locke, as well as his failure to follow the dictates of the national Klan, brought an end to the organization's power in Colorado. Locke broke away from the Klan and founded the Minute Men, which proved to be much less popular.

On the demise of the Klan, Stapleton denounced it but had accepted its support; and although he had eschewed its bigotry, he had also supported the election of Klansmen to city offices in 1923 and 1924. Perhaps it was also this kind of political expediency—or out of frustration after decades of reform work, or fear of the growing immigrant population and the failure of assimilation, or the need to recapture the power and notoriety of earlier years as a reformer—that a federated clubwoman of Denver was one of three who incorporated a Klan group for women.[7] In December 1924, Meta L. Gremmels, Dr. Ester B. Hunt, and Laurena H. Senter filed incorporation papers with the secretary of state for the Women of the Ku Klux Klan. The objects of the organization were

> the procuring and enforcement of just and equitable laws, upholding the constitution of the United States and the state of Colorado, teaching of respect for laws and law-enforcing authorities, furtherance of American principles, ideals and institutions, and relief work to alleviate suffering and distress.[8]

Only white women over eighteen years of age were eligible for membership in this Klan women's group. Senter, a member of the Woman's Club of Denver, became Imperial Commander of the Denver Klan No. One; Dr. Minnie C. T. Love became Excellent Commander.[9] Senter had attended public schools in Lincoln, Nebraska, before her family moved to Denver, where she graduated from high school. Later she attended Barnes Business School and the University of Denver. Love was well known in Denver as a suffragist, past member of the state board of charities and corrections, organizer of the State Industrial School for Girls and member of its board of control, the chief of the medical staff at the Crittenton Home, and one of the incorporators of Children's Hospital.[10] In 1921 she was elected to the state legislature. There, as a Klanswoman, she introduced legislation authorizing "the sterilization of epileptics, the retarded, and the insane if procreation might result in defective or feeble-minded children with criminal tendencies," as well as a bill advocating the distribution of birth control information and the manufacture and distribution of contraceptives.[11] Neither bill passed.

The dissension that shattered the men's organization also affected the women's Klan of Denver. Senter tried to steer a neutral course between the Klan and Locke's new Minute Men with a parade of unity in Arvada.[12] But when KKK Excellent Commander Minnie Love, also a lieutenant in the Minute Women, convinced a majority of Denver's 1,000 Klanswomen to shed hoods for Betsy Ross outfits, Senter suspended Love, revoked the Denver charter, and seized its assets to prevent their disappearance into Minute Women coffers. The Minute Women responded with a lawsuit. Although not successful, the lawsuit and rebellion in the women's Klan led to its destruction.[13]

Although regarded as an insidious movement by later generations, the Klan, according to Goldberg, offered hope and change to many people and thus received either their active support or neutrality.[14] Similarly, Robert G. Athearn in *The Coloradans* also makes the case that the Colorado Klan

> was a harmless manifestation of the juvenile desire to participate in uniformed parades and to chant mindless slogans, an activity not unknown to Americans in other and less offensive organizations. Under the guise of patriotism it provided an opportunity for men and women to take emotional shelter in an exclusive, secret social group at a time of national and local unrest.[15]

But the activities of the Klan were not restricted to marching and chanting. How involved the Klanswomen were in fueling the flames of bigotry and in harassing minorities is difficult to say. From contemporary newspaper accounts, the women appear to have served as little more than an honorary women's auxiliary concerned with such tasks as distributing food to needy families.[16]

Aside from the aberration of Klan involvement, clubwomen of Denver during the 1920s continued with their regular philanthropic work. They gave money to the Colorado Federation, the Scholarship Fund, Denver General Hospital maternity ward, the Sands Home for tubercular patients, and the Florence Crittenton Home. They bought magazine subscriptions or provided entertainment for the State Industrial schools for boys and girls, the Old Ladies' Home, and the YWCA. Two clubs, the Fortnightly and Monday Literary clubs, refurnished their rooms at the YWCA Rest and Recreation center—the first in honor of member Ella Vincent, who died in 1920. The Twenty-Second Avenue Study Club sent books to the Traveling Library and developed a friendship bag to send to children in Mexico. Both the Woman's Club of Denver and the North Side Women's Club supplied clothing for victims of the Pueblo flood in 1921. The Fortnightly Club was honored with a life membership to the State Historical Society in recognition of its contributions over the years to the Society.[17]

In legislation, the clubs took up various causes. They endorsed the Kellogg-Briand Pact outlawing war; endorsed a bill providing for a psychiatric ward at Colorado General Hospital; protested the city's industrial smoke and the failure to enforce pollution laws; supported a maternity bill under debate in the United States Senate; endorsed a child labor bill in the Colorado General Assembly; advocated a law prohibiting the use of women in tobacco ads on billboards; and supported a measure providing for a minimum salary for teachers.

IN OCTOBER 1929, the nation's financial house of cards came crashing down with the collapse of the stock market. By 1932 nearly one in four Americans were without jobs. Thousands of people began to wander around the country looking for work. The suffering of the farmers, who had not experienced the good times of the 1920s, worsened when serious drought and wind turned the southern Great Plains into a dust bowl.

As the nation plunged deeper into depression, the federated clubwomen continued on as well as could be expected. Only a few clubs in the state disbanded, one deferred payment of dues, and several dropped out of the General and Colorado federations to save money.[18] Among these were the Monday Literary Club, which withdrew in 1930, and the Round Table Club, which withdrew in 1934.[19] In the meantime, these joined with the other four clubs to continue literary study, carry on their usual philanthropic work, and attempt to meet the needs of their community during these years of hardship.

In nearly all of the six clubs, the changing of the guard was complete by the middle of the 1930s. Three of the six clubs—the Fortnightly, the Monday Literary, and the Woman's Club—had no living charter members after 1930, while in the Round Table Club, only El Frieda Whiteman remained from the 1895 roster. The Twenty-Second Avenue Study Club, with five of its original twenty-five members and an average of thirty members throughout the decades, was the most stable. Once considered the most elite of the Denver clubs, its remaining "old members" were Maude Weisser, Mary Hiatt, Alice G. Henry, Christine Duling, and Alice H. Bartlett.[20] Nettie E. Caspar, president of the club from its founding to 1924, died in 1932—a big loss not only for the Twenty-Second Avenue but also for the Woman's Club and the Monday Literary Club.[21]

In 1930 the Fortnightly Club lost two charter members, Lavinia Spalding and Susan Riley Ashley, as well as Mary Francis Fisher, a member since 1893. Twelve new members were added to this club during the 1930s, most notably Dr. Florence R. Sabin in 1938. Besides Nettie Caspar, the Monday Literary Club lost Ida Winne Ballantine, who committed suicide in 1934 by leaping from the fire escape of her hotel,[22] and Alice B. Humphreys. During the decade, nine new members were added. A plan to increase the club's membership to thirty-five was voted down, even though attendance at meetings was chronically low.[23]

Both of the large departmental clubs—the Woman's Club and the North Side Women's Club—experienced declines in membership during the first five years of the 1930s. Membership in the first dropped from 240 in 1930 to 182 in 1934; the second fell from 176 in 1931 to 133 in 1935 and to 115 in 1939. Only 22 of those North Side Club losses were due to death. By mid-decade, only 6 charter members remained and 53 of the current members had been on the roster since 1925.[24] The Woman's Club lost charter members Honora MacPherson (president, 1920–22), Mary C. C. Bradford, and Nettie E. Caspar, and members Helen Grenfell and Lucile Jorndt (president, 1932–34). The club, however, drastically increased its membership after 1935. Within three years, membership totaled 337, a jump of 85 percent. This was undoubtedly the result of president Senter's active recruiting process.[25]

Just as they had since the 1880s and 1890s, the clubwomen mixed program topics of general or literary interest with issues relevant to the time, such as national defense, the history of the tariff, social insurance, the effects of the "Russian situation" on America, and the impact of radio. The Monday Literary Club, in addition to offering its regular-fare novelists, essayists, and poets, undertook to determine the twelve greatest living women.[26] "Undisputed," states its yearbook, "were Helen Keller, Jane Addams, Willa Cather, Grace Abbott, Carrie Chapman Catt, and Mademoiselle Schumann-Heink." More debatable—but worthy of consideration—were Annie Besant, Madame Curie, Emma Goldman, Edna St. Vincent Millay, and Margaret Sanger. A twelfth apparently could not be found.

The hardships occasioned by the Great Depression meant that the philanthropic work of the Denver clubs was needed more than ever. Throughout the decade members of the Twenty-Second Avenue Study Club donated money, food, clothing, and quilts to the Florence Crittenton Home, Fitzsimons Hospital, Pantry Shelf, and Red Cross.[27] Similarly, the Woman's Club, through its committees, tried to help those in need. The American Home Committee, for example, made over 2,600 garments, sent books to the state penitentiary, and opened a sewing room in conjunction with the Employment Committee of the City and County of Denver. To help its own members, the club lowered dues and decided no longer to allow the free use of its clubhouse to other groups "so that the welfare of the Club would not be impaired."[28] It also replaced its drama committee with one devoted to health, from which members who were doctors gave their services and medical care to indigent women and children.[29]

The North Side Woman's Club, like the others, donated cans to the Pantry Shelf, money to the Colorado Federation scholarship fund, sewing to the Red Cross, garments and money to the Florence Crittenton Home, the Sands Home, and the Ladies' Relief Home, and contributions to the Denver Civic Symphony Society, the Denver Art Museum, and Fitzsimons Hospital. This club also took an active part in the National Recovery Act drive in September 1933.[30]

The twenty years between the two world wars was a time of change in the makeup of the clubs and in the lack of any new involvement. As older members died or passed to inactive, honorary status, the work of the clubs centered around projects which had been initiated in the early years. Even the advent of the Great Depression stimulated no new directions within the clubs' work; it only meant a greater need for the services they had always performed—aid to the needy and disadvantaged. World War II would bring a return to the war service efforts, and this time club leadership would be provided by the newer members.

THE WORLD WAR II YEARS, 1941-1945

D URING WORLD WAR I, Denver's clubwomen provided the most important female wartime leadership in the state and city. Appointed to the Council of Defense, leading Liberty Loan Drives, or heading Red Cross campaigns, clubwomen ably mobilized and directed large numbers of both clubwomen and non-clubwomen for the war effort. By 1940, however, the leaders of 1917 were either dead or no longer taking an active role in community and state affairs, and the new leaders were not as well known outside the club world as their 1917 predecessors had been.

For twenty years, the clubs had been quietly continuing with their philanthropic work and literary study. No massive projects had been undertaken at the local or state levels to bring clubwomen to the attention of the city's leaders. Woman suffrage, employment bureaus, day nurseries, and protective legislation for children and women had been largely secured decades before. While still supportive of state institutions and local charities, the clubwomen had become less visible to those outside the club world. Thus, when Governor Ralph Carr named nearly two hundred citizens for a state defense council, not one clubwoman was included on the list.[1] While this omission does not imply that clubwomen were any less active in the service to their country during the Second World War than they were in the First, it does show that they were less visible as leaders.

During World War II the customary balance of interest that clubs maintained between general topics and socially relevant topics shifted subtly toward the latter. As if to signal a change, Dr. Florence Sabin, who had joined the Fortnightly Club in 1938, broke with tradition to present her topics extemporaneously. A graduate of Smith College and Johns Hopkins Medical School, Sabin had returned to her native state of Colorado after having spent thirteen years as a member of the Rockefeller Institute for Medical Research.[2] For the Fortnightly, she spoke about epidemics and progress in public health. Other club papers of the war period included "Winston Churchill and His Parents,"

"Europe in 1937," "Foreign Policy," "Women and the War effort," and "Lend-Lease."[3]

Although the Twenty-Second Avenue Study Club discussed miscellaneous topics in the early years of the war, by mid-decade it held five-minute talks each meeting on war, peace, home, and women. "Women in Defense" talks included the armed forces, industry, Citizens for Victory, and American Voluntary Services.[4] Likewise, the North Side Women's Club dealt with the war and its related topics.[5]

Because the women were once again preoccupied with war service work, the Denver clubs maintained their usual contributions and did not attempt any new undertakings. The State Industrial School for Girls, the State Industrial School for Boys, the Old Ladies' Home, and the YWCA Rest and Recreation Rooms received attention and care from the clubwomen. And although war rationing caused problems, the Twenty-Second Avenue Study Club continued with its luncheons at the Adult Workshop for the Blind:

> The main dishes arrived in the arms of their cooks . . . and spaghetti and meatballs, noodles and tuna fish, scalloped potatoes and hot rolls, gave our guests the "something hot and hearty" that tastes so good to the lunch-box enslaved worker. Home-made jelly and cold slaw [sic] for relishes, applesauce and doughnuts for dessert, with plenty of hot coffee, was not hard to take, judging by the expressions and comments. Mrs. Gifford asked the blessing, and club members helped them when necessary. It is certainly touching—and humbling to the spirit—to see how cheerful and capable these people are.[6]

The luncheon was followed by entertainment by the blind men and women. The following year the club served veal balls and spaghetti since veal was "low-cost in red points."[7]

In 1943, the Twenty-Second Avenue Study Club received an appeal for an endorsement, this time for the Equal Rights Amendment to the United States Constitution. Although it was approved with only one dissenting vote, the dissenter, as historian, left her opinions in the club histories for posterity:

Business session brought an appeal for endorsement of what is known as the Equal Rights Amendment to the U.S. Constitution. (Why on Earth do club women, whose lives have very seldom given them any actual contact with working conditions, insist on supporting this monstrosity, anathema to every working woman?)[8]

Lucile Kling, who was the writer and club historian, also decried the club's endorsement a month later and referred to the secretary's job of notifying senators and representatives of the club's support of the amendment as a "task."[9] She was no more enthusiastic when the club "joined the rising chorus demanding women jurors—and obtained the rather doubtful privilege of jury duty."[10]

Although not appointed to the kinds of war-related committees and agencies that their predecessors had been during World War I, the clubwomen of Denver were important members of, and workers for, World War II organizations. They bought and sold war bonds, participated in numerous drives and campaigns, taught classes, provided entertainment to the soldiers, and supported the efforts of the Red Cross in every way. The Colorado Federation of Women's Clubs reported that clubwomen in the state had bought $97,000 in bonds and stamps during the war and had sold over $200,000.[11] The North Side Woman's Club alone reported that its members had bought $7,000 in bonds by 1942.[12]

Clubwomen also participated in nearly every drive or campaign. In 1941 they donated to "Bundles for Britain," collected food and clothing for two victory drives, and gave books to the Victory Book Campaign. The Women's Division of the Greek Civilian War Relief Drive exceeded its quota of $2,500 thanks to the efforts of Denver clubwomen.[13] The clubhouse of the Woman's Club of Denver, which had been set aside during World War I as a servicemen's center, was now loaned to the government for draft registration.[14] Red Cross membership and blood donor drives were also supported by the clubwomen, who joined both organizations, canvassed neighborhoods for new members and blood donors, and regularly donated blood themselves. And, just as they had during the earlier war, clubwomen held and attended classes on home nursing, first aid, and nutrition.

In response to the suffering caused by the war, Denver women also supported Russian relief in particular by making layettes for Russian women's babies.[15] The women of the Twenty-Second Avenue Study Club took up a collection to buy material for their proposed layette, which was later chosen as one of five to be exhibited at the Russian War Relief rally held at the City Auditorium.[16] The same clubwomen were also interested in the salvage operations of the American Women's Voluntary Services, of which their own Jennie Steidley served as chair.[17] In 1943 Denver women turned in 500,000 pounds of old stockings and 540 tons of tin cans to the salvage bureau located at 139 Fifteenth Street.[18] Steidley later received a United States Treasury citation for her war work.[19] In addition to nylon and tin cans, the women of the club salvaged over one hundred pounds of fats during the club year 1945-46.[20]

Denver, with its military bases and hospitals and within a day's drive of other military installations in the state, was a rest and recreation center for thousands of soldiers. Prior to World War II, city boosters had attracted Fitzsimons Hospital, Lowry Field, and Fort Logan. In 1942 Buckley Naval Air Station was constructed just east of the city. Camp Carson, which was south of Colorado Springs, and Camp Hale, established near Leadville to train special mountain troops, were both established in the 1940s.[21] Thus, Denver was the site of many free nights and weekend passes for thousands of soldiers. American communities did not fare well under such onslaughts, but Denver adjusted well. In fact, in July 1943, *Business Week* dubbed the city a "Good Neighbor."[22]

Credit for such a reputation must go to the planning of the city leaders and the work and hospitality of the citizens, many of whom were clubwomen. These women distributed gifts to the Fort Logan convalescent ward, gave books and playing cards to the USO, and entertained recuperating soldiers at Fitzsimons Hospital. The board of the Woman's Club of Denver passed a resolution that each member should entertain at least two soldiers a month. Many did that and more.[23] For the USO "March of Cookies," the Twenty-Second Avenue Study Club baked sixty-two dozen cookies in 1944-45 and another forty-nine dozen during 1945-46.[24] This club also took old Christmas cards, made their own envelopes, and distributed holiday greetings to patients at the area hospitals. By 1943 over 1,200 cards had been given to soldiers who were alone for the holidays.[25]

Besides working through their clubs for the war effort, clubwomen acted individually to help ease the loneliness of the soldiers. Zimmie Rupp, for example, regularly met servicemen's visiting wives at the train station and placed soldiers who were on leave in the homes of her friends. She and her husband Otto would invite servicemen over for Sunday dinners and use the Red Point coupons her sister sent her to place enough meat on the table. Their kindness obviously touched the men, for over the years she received Christmas cards from many of them.[26]

In 1943 the Colorado Federation participated in a novel project for World War II. This was the "Buy a Bomber" campaign. The federated clubs in the state raised enough money to purchase one heavy bomber named for the Federation, nine pursuit planes—one for each district—one complete mobile laundry unit, and two motor scooters with side cars.[27]

While the clubwomen bought and sold bonds, entertained soldiers, collected food and clothing for victims of the war, and salvaged tin cans and stockings, they constantly worked for the Red Cross. The War Fund campaigns had begun in Denver in 1940. By 1945 the Denver Red Cross chapter had 74 paid staff members and over 13,000 volunteers. The organization, first housed at 300 East Eighth Avenue, later moved to the Claude Boettcher Mansion at 800 Logan Street when its original quarters became too cramped. The Red Cross also used the basement of the Grant-Humphreys Mansion, community centers, and, of course, the clubhouse of the Woman's Club.[28] All the Denver clubs participated in the membership drives and blood donor drives of the Red Cross. In addition, many members donated blood themselves on a regular basis and club treasuries gave money to the Denver chapter. The North Side Woman's Club members made fifty garments, five afghans, fourteen lap robes for recuperating soldiers, thirty pairs of slippers, and twenty-three turtleneck sweaters for the Red Cross between 1942 and 1944.[29] Much of this work was done during club meetings.

In the Twenty-Second Avenue Study Club, the women met every other Wednesday through the club year to sew for the Red Cross. They would arrive between 10:00 A.M. and noon, sew until breaking for a lunch of sandwiches, hold a meeting at 2:00 P.M., and adjourn at 4:00 P.M.—"otherwise all of us can just stand on the corner and watch car after crowded car go snorting by! War workers care not at all whether mere club members ever get home!"[30] Lunch discussion generally centered around the women's canning work—what, how much, and how. In the fourteen informal meetings between spring and fall 1943, the clubwomen contributed 784 hours of labor to the Red Cross. Under the leadership of their Red Cross Committee chair, Dorothy Read, they provided buddy bags, slumber robes, nightshirts, and diapers. The report of their Red Cross sewing activity for 1943–44 shows graphically the productivity and dedication of these clubwomen: 620 articles were made; 120 yards of tape were dyed, pressed, and rolled; 24 sewing meetings were attended; and 1,759 hours were spent on sewing work.[31] Even as the war was drawing to a close, this club spent 237 hours making housewife kits.[32]

In spite of, or perhaps because of, their war service work, clubwomen remained loyal and dedicated to their organizations. With the exception of the Woman's Club of Denver, which as usual experienced fluctuations in membership, the Denver clubs maintained continuity. Death, however, struck women in a number of clubs, among them the Fortnightly's Ella S. Denison in 1940. Denison had founded the club in 1881, had been its president from 1924 to 1925, and had been active in civic affairs. In 1887 she helped form the Denver YWCA, and in 1896 she helped organize the Civil Service Reform League and the City Improvement Society. She served as president of the Old Ladies' Home in 1900 and for four years (1921–25) was a member of the school board. During the First World War, she headed one of the departments of the Mountain Division of the American Red Cross. One of her enduring legacies was the Denison Memorial Research Laboratories at the University of Colorado School of Medicine, founded in memory of her son, Dr. Henry Strong Denison, who died in 1912.[33]

During the war years the Monday Literary Club maintained

its high percentage of attendance at meetings, its membership at around thirty, and a membership longevity of over twenty years for more than half of its members. Death, however, struck this club as well, claiming Sue McCrary (president 1918–19), Phoebe McAllister (a member from 1910 to 1944 and president from 1921 to 1922), and Leila Kinney (a member since 1916 and president from 1930 to 1931). Eva LeFevre (1896), Sarah T. Arneill (1907), Eva Miller (1909), and Obie P. Dunklee (1924) were four of the women with the greatest longevity.[34] Virginia M. Shafroth, who had been a member since 1907 and president from 1924 to 1925, resigned from active status in 1945, but not before being honored as Colorado's first "Golden Rule Mother."[35] As was club tradition, the women did not accept Shafroth's resignation from the club; she was placed on the honorary list.

The Round Table Club suffered seven deaths between 1940 and 1945,[36] and clubwomen of the Twenty-Second Avenue Study Club were saddened by the deaths of four of the remaining five original members: Alice G. Henry, Alice H. Bartlett, Christine W. Duling, and Mary Hiatt.[37] (Hiatt's role as historian was given to Lucille Kling, the daughter of another charter member, Adelle E. Kling.) Another death in this club, later in the decade, was Florence Sargent. A schoolteacher, Sargent had worked hard for conservation while a clubwoman. During the war, an acre of young spruce trees were set aside in the National Reserve and christened the "Florence Sargent Acre" in recognition of her work to save Colorado's trees and flowers.[38]

Membership in the Woman's Club of Denver fluctuated from 413 in 1940 to 372 in 1942, then rose again to 493 in 1945. Club records do not indicate a reason for this fluctuation, except that it was usual for the club to gain and lose large numbers of members. Two past presidents were among the many deaths between 1940 and 1944. Lionna F. Jeancon was a member from 1922 to her death in 1944 and club president from 1940 to 1942. Very active in the state federation, Jeancon served as corresponding secretary, parliamentarian, and president of the club's central district, which consisted of the Denver metropolitan region. She was nationally recognized as an authority on parliamentary procedure, having written several magazine articles and pamphlets on the subject.[39] Another Woman's Club member, active in other clubs, who died during World War II was Minnie Lorena Weir. A Canadian by birth, Weir had served as treasurer (1913–14) and president (1918–20) of the Woman's Club, as secretary of the Historic Art Club (1913–14), and as president of the Fourth Avenue Club (1911–13).[40]

Between 1940 and 1945, twenty members of the North Side Woman's Club died, among them three charter members, including Mary L. Parks, who had been president from 1904 to 1906. By the end of the war, only four charter members remained. Another death during the war years was Tida Z. Hilliard, the wife of a Colorado Supreme Court justice.

Between the two world wars, the clubwomen of Denver concentrated on projects begun before 1914 and on legislative matters which had not yet been passed into law. While the work of the clubs was valuable, it had none of the fanfare and publicity of earlier years. Following the lead of the state federation, the clubs continued with their studies and philanthropic endeavors, drawing no criticism or even much notice. The invisibility of twenty years left clubwomen outside of leadership roles in the wartime home-front agencies, but not without responsibilities. Mobilizing and working just as diligently for their country in World War II as they had twenty-five years earlier, the clubwomen of Denver made a positive impact on the community and the servicemen and women stationed in the city.

CONCLUSION

I N THE TWO DECADES following World War II, the Denver clubs remained fairly constant in the membership totals. Present members remained active, there were few deaths, and no new members were admitted. By 1965, however, this pattern of postwar stability was changing. Combined with an absence of new members, normal attrition had begun to reduce club membership drastically. During the 1920s clubs had also experienced a large generational turnover, but efforts to recruit new members had kept the club world vital. During the 1960s, on the other hand—and throughout the 1970s and 1980s—social changes in American life, in addition to club policies and practices themselves, sharply reduced the impact of women's clubs, if not their effectiveness.

American society has obviously undergone massive change in the past forty years. Women now constitute a large part of the labor force, Americans are more mobile than they ever were before, the number of volunteer charitable organizations has expanded, and the federal government has become much more involved in social welfare. These four changes have drastically affected the federated clubs. Many women, working outside the home, do not have the time or energy to spend on literary study and philanthropic projects, even if they had the desire. For some women, dropping a tax-deductible check in the mail for a favorite charity is much less time-consuming than actively participating in a volunteer organization.

Another change in the United States in the past forty years has been the great mobility of its people. Those who are accustomed to moving often do not tie themselves to local organizations—or as readily as they might have done in the past. In the 1920s, for instance, Zimmie Rupp joined the Twenty-Second Avenue Study Club at the invitation of a neighbor, and she remained active in the club from that time on—even serving as president for three terms. These casual and neighborly contacts at home, at the grocery store, and at church offered ample prospects for securing future club members. Today's high mobility and the lack of traditional neighborliness has contributed to the clubs' failure to recruit new members.

A third change in American society affecting the decline in women's clubs has been the proliferation of social, professional, and volunteer organizations to which women may belong or contribute. Professional organizations for career women include the Society of Women Engineers, the Business Professional Women, the Women's Society of Certified Public Accountants, Women in Architecture, the National Education Association, and the Women Business Owners Association. Fraternal organizations include the Order of Eastern Star, Job's Daughters, and Rainbow Girls as well as other women's auxiliaries to men's fraternal organizations. Church organizations abound for women and have always offered a place for those who are interested in charitable work or study. For those who wish to become involved in feminist activities, local chapters of the National Organization for Women exist in most cities, while local chapters of the League of Women Voters offer substantial opportunities for politically minded women.[1] Another important charitable organization in Denver is the Junior League, founded in 1918, whose philanthropic activities include the Needlework Guild, the Children's Theatre, Rude Park Community Center, and the Children's Museum. These are but a few of the organizations for women made up of women.

In addition to organizations for women are dozens of others in which women play an important part as volunteers or paid staff. A small sampling includes Big Sisters, Gray Panthers, People Who Need People, Girl Scouts, Camp Fire Girls, Youth Challenge, and the Red Cross. In Denver, organizations for the arts and cultural appreciation flourish: The Central City Opera House Association, Metropolitan Denver Arts Alliance, the Denver Art Museum Association, the Denver Symphony Guild, the Colorado Historical Society, and Historic Denver, Inc.

If a woman has a particular interest and is pressed for time, an organization which specifically deals with her interest, whether that be religious, civic, feminist, artistic, historical, or ethnic, is more likely to receive her membership and support. The federated clubs, while being of great service to many people through diverse projects and programs, are perhaps too broad in their sweep to interest women who wish to channel their energies toward one specific goal or area of concern. Thus, women's clubs have lost ground to vast numbers of other organizations, each serving certain segments of society and accomplishing much in their area.

Prior to the Great Depression, the different levels of government in the United States were not seriously involved in social welfare. The New Deal programs of Franklin D. Roosevelt, however, brought about considerable change. There are now countless bureaus and departments at the municipal, state, and national level designed to protect, educate, treat, investigate, and develop American citizens, their ills, and their skills. At first, the government adopted the programs begun by women's clubs and other organizations; later, in response to the Depression, the Second World War, and the changes in American life since then, these few multiplied profusely until they cover nearly every aspect of one's life from birth to death.

Thus, many of the roles that women's clubs played in American society during the 1880s and the 1890s have been adopted by other volunteer organizations and by various governmental agencies and bureaus. The skills of self-confidence, research, public speaking, and politics that the early clubwomen developed in their literary study and philanthropic work are now being developed in colleges and universities, in networking groups, in civic organizations, and on the job.

This is not to say that the purpose of the federated clubs has passed; the work which they do is still very important. However, as more women enter the labor force, as Americans become more mobile, as competing organizations are formed, and as government becomes more involved in social welfare, women's clubs have inevitably lost the position they once held as social instruments of philanthropic work. Once they held the mantle for social welfare; now, they are but one of many organizations intensely involved in improving people's lives.

ABBREVIATIONS USED

CFWC Colorado Federation of
       Women's Clubs
DFC   Denver Fortnightly Club
DPL   Western History Department,
       Denver Public Library
GFWC General Federation of
       Women's Clubs
MLC   Monday Literary Club
NSWC North Side Women's Club
RTC   Round Table Club
TASC   Twenty-Second Avenue
       Study Club
WCD   Woman's Club of Denver

Introduction

1
Karen J. Blair, *The Clubwoman as Feminist: True Womanhood Redefined, 1868–1914* (New York: Holmes & Meier Publishers, Inc., 1980), 15, 31.

2
The General Federation of Women's Clubs was founded for the clubs of white women. However, as described in this volume by Lynda Dickson, black women also formed clubs to work for the moral, economic, social, and religious welfare of women and children in their communities. Gerda Lerner, in *The Majority Finds Its Past: Placing Women in History* (New York: Oxford University Press, 1979), discusses the beginnings of local black clubs in the 1890s and the founding of the National Association of Colored Women in 1896. Organizers included Ida B. Wells, Josephine St. Pierre Ruffin, and Mary Church Terrell, who said that the success of the white women's club movement influenced them. In Colorado, the Federation of Colored Women's Clubs of Colorado was founded by Elizabeth Piper Ensley of Colorado Springs in 1903. The Denver Club established the George Washington Carver Day Nursery at Twenty-fourth Avenue and Clarkson Street in 1916. This was later taken over by the Commu-

nity Chest and then by the Mile High Chapter of the United Way. See papers of the Colorado Colored Women's Clubs in the Western History Collection at the Denver Public Library.

3
Jane Cunningham Croly, *The History of the Women's Club Movement in America, 1868–1898* (New York: Henry G. Allen & Company, 1898), 98.

4
Blair, *The Clubwoman as Feminist*, 22.

5
Edward T. James, ed., *Notable American Women* (Cambridge: Belknap Press, 1971), 410.

6
Some Denver families sent their children back east to school (see letters between Margaret Patterson Campbell and her daughter Katharine in the family papers of Thomas M. Patterson at Norlin Library, Western History Collection, University of Colorado, Boulder). The minutes of the MLC from 1903 to 1908 mention that the first meeting in October was for "vacation story" papers. Trips mentioned were to California, Europe, Vermont, and just "back East."

7
Blair, *The Clubwoman as Feminist*, 453. An examination of the Denver clubs' minutes bears out this generalization: All prospective candidates were favorably voted on in the meeting of the board of directors or executive council and then voted in by the general membership. The only evidence to the contrary is that in the DFC some candidates for membership were dropped and never brought to a vote because the women smoked.

8
Ibid., 23. Croly discouraged discussion of suffrage and religion in the clubs because she felt that those two

issues, as controversial as they were, would possibly divide club members and cause a split in the ranks. A split would hamper the women's true mission—challenging injustice. It was only suffrage and religious discussions that she wished to avoid. Frank discussions of injustices of the day—such as child labor, education, and government abuses—were encouraged. The DFC also agreed not to discuss suffrage. The name for Croly's club, Sorosis, refers to plants with an aggregation of flowers that bore fruit (ibid., 21). Names for Denver clubs include: Sphinx Club, Clio Club, Entre Nous, Fourth Avenue Club, Friday Morning Club, and Reviewers Club.

9
Mildred White Wells, *Unity in Diversity*, vol. 2 (Washington, D.C.: General Federation of Women's Clubs, 1975), 3: "Some four-fifths of the public libraries in the United States were started originally by women's clubs and many clubs still maintain the only public library in their community."

10
Interview with Zelma ("Zimmie") Rupp, TASC, Denver, Colorado, August 15, 1986. Rupp served as a past and current president, and member of this club since 1926.

11
Neata M. Preiss, *The Colorado Federation of Women's Clubs Seventy-fifth Anniversary Edition, 1895–1970* (Denver: Colorado Federation of Women's Clubs, 1970), 12.

12
Jeannette Bain, *History and Chronology of the Colorado State Federation of Women's Clubs, 1895–1955* (Denver: Colorado Federation of Women's Clubs, 1955), 6.

13
Preiss, *The Colorado Federation*, 11.

14
Lowry Rev-Meter, February 11, 1944.

The Early Years

1
Lyle W. Dorsett, *The Queen City: A History of Denver* (Boulder: Pruett Publishing Co., 1977), 57.

2
Ibid., 60.

3
Ibid., 44–45.

4
Ibid., 46.

5
Mary Caroline Bancroft, "A Retrospective Sketch of the Fortnightly Club, 1881–1888" (Denver, 1888), WH108, DPL.

6
Susan Riley Ashley, "A Very Brief Chronicle of the Denver Fortnightly's First Thirty-five Years" (Denver, 1916), WH108, DPL.

7
Yearbooks of the Denver Fortnightly Club [hereinafter DFC yearbooks], 1895–1900.

8
Of particular note: Ella Denison's husband, Charles, was a well-known tuberculosis physician; Susan R. Ashley's husband, Eli M., had been secretary of state under Territorial Governor John Evans; Lavinia Spalding's husband, John F., was bishop of Wyoming and Colorado; Margaret Gray Evans's husband was Colorado's second territorial governor; and Mary Kountze's husband, Charles, was co-founder of the Colorado National Bank.

9
Of the thirty-seven women who

were no longer with the DFC in 1916, eighteen had died, thirteen had moved away from Denver, and six had resigned. By the end of World War I, 36 percent of the current members had been in the club over twenty years and 41 percent less than ten years.

10
Carla Swan Coleman, "The Turn of the Century" (Denver, 1971), WH108, DPL.

11
The Wolcott School, No. 12 (Denver, 1909).

12
Mabel Mann Runnette, "In a Changing World," vol. 1 (Denver, 1935), WH317, DPL.

13
MLC yearbooks, 1893–1900.

14
MLC minutes, 1887.

15
Born on December 16, 1843, in Sandy Hill, New York, Bates was graduated from Fort Edward Collegiate Institute and Northwestern Women's College. She received her medical training at the Women's Medical College of Pennsylvania and married George C. Bates, an attorney, in 1877. He died in 1885, four years after she opened her medical office. Her philanthropic activities included serving six years on the Denver Board of Education and, as stated in the text, helping to establish Denver's early medical dispensary. She remained a life member of the MLC until her death in 1924.

16
Nettie Caspar, a graduate of Lake Erie College, was a founder and president of the TASC, a member of the MLC since 1896, and president of the MLC from 1907 to 1908.

17
Mary Dunklee was graduated from St. Johnsbury Academy (Vermont) before becoming a teacher in Trinidad, Colorado. After her marriage in 1883, she taught at Gilpin School in Denver. Later she wrote books of poetry, was an MLC president (1908–9), and a member of the WCD.

18
Wixson, a member of the MLC, WCD, and the Denver Woman's Press Club in the 1890s, became state superintendent of public instruction in 1909, a position she held for four years (*Rocky Mountain News*, April 23, 1925).

19
A graduate of Wellesley College, Robinson taught at Wolfe Hall and at Wolcott School. As president of the Denver Woman's Press Club and the MLC, and as speaker for the United States Suffrage Association, she gained many supporters and admirers. As a state senator she became known as the spokeswoman for women and children in the legislature (*Denver Republican*, November 8, 1912).

20
Arneill was also a member of the Colorado Equal Suffrage Association, the Colorado Chapter of the DAR, the Drama League, the Government Science Club, and the National Congress of Mothers, of which she became vice president in 1910.

21
LeFevre, an 1871 graduate of Ohio Wesleyan, belonged to the Artists' Club, the Denver Woman's Press Club, and the American Association of University Women. She had done previous philanthropic work through the Ladies' Relief Society and had served as the first secretary of the board of Miss Wolcott's School in Denver.

22
The wife of Henry McAllister, an attorney and counsel for the Denver and Rio Grande Western Railway, Phoebe McAllister ("Gussie" to her friends) belonged to the Reviewers' Club and the Woman's Union for Political Action as well as serving as MLC president from 1921 to 1922. The McAllister home, now known as the Pearce-McAllister Cottage, at 1880 Gaylord in Denver, is designated an official Denver Landmark and is listed in the National Register of Historic Places. Of Dutch Colonial architecture, it is presently a house museum owned by the Colorado Historical Society.

23
Virginia Morrison, after graduation from Howard Payne College, taught school in Missouri prior to marrying John Franklin Shafroth in 1881. That same year, she helped to organize the RTC. Later club memberships included the MLC, Mittwoch, Daughters of the American Revolution, and the WCD. Her husband was a city attorney and later served as a member of the U.S. House of Representatives, as state governor, and as U.S. senator.

24
Margaret Patterson Campbell was the daughter of U.S. senator and *Rocky Mountain News* owner and publisher Thomas M. Patterson and his wife Katharine Grafton Patterson, herself a member of the WCD, the DFC, and the Colorado Equal Suffrage Association. A graduate of Denver's East High School and Bryn Mawr College, Margaret Patterson married Richard Crawford Campbell, the business manager of the *Rocky Mountain News*. Following in her active mother's footsteps, she belonged to the DFC, the MLC, the WCD, Der Deutsche Damen, the Woman's Press Club, the Drama League of America, and the Colorado branch of the Association of Collegiate Alumnae.

25
Elisabeth Spalding, who joined the MLC in 1916, was an accomplished painter and one of the founders of the Denver Artists' Club. She was also president of the DFC from 1925 to 1926. She died in 1954, having never married. Her younger sister, Sarah Griswold Spalding, joined DFC in 1940. An 1896 graduate of Vassar College, Sarah Spalding was assistant headmistress of Madeira School for over twenty years before retiring in 1939. Besides being DFC president from 1947 to 1948, she devoted a great deal of time and energy to Saint John's Cathedral and to Saint Luke's Hospital.

26
Named Colorado's poet laureate in 1919, Alice Polk Hill taught music, was a newspaper correspondent, and wrote two books. She was a charter member of the RTC, WCD, Woman's Press Club, DAR, Daughters of the Confederacy, the League of American Pen Women, and the State Historical and Natural History Society of Colorado (Alice Polk Hill Papers, Denver).

27
Denver City Directory, 1895 [hereinafter DCD]. Records for the RTC are scanty. The earliest extant yearbook is for 1895–96 and, as with all the club's records, only the husband's first name is given. While many clubs made it a practice to list the first names of both spouses, as late as 1980 (the latest yearbook available) the RTC still did not list the woman's. As for the members' marital status, in 1895 only two of the twenty-two members of the RTC were single—a proportion that still held up twenty-two years later, when two out of thirty-one were single. Of these latter two women, one was a schoolteacher and the other, Alverta Ellis, was listed in the DCD as having no occupation outside the home.

28
Besides Alice Polk Hill, other recognized club leaders included Josephine Seifried, Florence McCrea, Emma Miller, and Mrs. Fred C. Shaw.

29
RTC minutes, 1891–1921.

30
See Helen Cannon, "First Ladies of Colorado: Mary Thompson McCook," *The Colorado Magazine* 39 (July 1962): 179–84.

31
Mary E. Hiatt, "History of the Twenty-Second Avenue Study Club, 1893–1934," MS965, Colorado Historical Society, Denver.

32
Ibid. There is no mention in the history as to why some members of the suffrage league did not join the study club.

33
Among these twenty-five were two mothers and daughters: Louisa Hiatt and her unmarried daughter, Mary E., and Christine Duling and her daughter, Maude D. Weisser. Mary Hiatt never married, was the club historian, and was the last surviving charter member. She died in the 1940s. Maude Weisser, who joined in 1898 with her mother, died in the 1960s after sixty-plus years of active membership.

34
The two single members were Ella Fee and Mary E. Hiatt. Fee moved to California but never married. Hiatt was a lifelong active member of the TASC. In an interview with Zimmie Rupp (May 20, 1987), a member since 1926, she stated that she never knew of any occupation for Mary Hiatt. Hiatt, however, felt that she knew Rupp well enough to entrust to her a brown dress she had worn the day the TASC was founded (Rupp interview, October 15, 1986).

35
Interview with Zimmie Rupp, October 15, 1986.

36
Cora V. Collett and Lisbeth G. Fish, comps., *History of the Woman's Club of Denver, 1894–1930* (Denver: The Woman's Club of Denver, 1930).

37
Ibid.

38
Born in 1852 in Vermont, Sarah Sophia Chase graduated from high school in Holyoke, Massachusetts. She and her second husband, James H. Platt, moved to Denver where he died in 1894. In 1899 she married Westbrook S. Decker, a well-known member of the Colorado bar.

39
Edward T. James, ed., *Notable American Women*, 451–52.

40
Ibid. See also *Denver Republican*, August 5, 1912. A branch of the Denver Public Library, the Sarah Platt Decker Branch Library at 1501 Logan Street, is named in honor of the suffragist, clubwoman, and reformer.

41
NSWC minutes, 1895–96.

42
NSWC yearbooks, 1895–1900.

43
Eleanor Flexner, *Century of Struggle: The Woman's Rights Movement in the United States* (Cambridge, Mass.: The Belknap Press of Harvard University Press, 1975), 183–84.

44
Collette and Fish, comps., *History of the Woman's Club*, p. 11.

45
Reformers in the WCD included:
Elizabeth Byers (who founded the
Ladies Union Aid Society and the
Working Boys' Home), Margaret P.
Campbell, Eliza F. Routt, Elizabeth
Iliff Warren (who helped form the
Denver Orphans' Home in 1872),
and Alice Hale Hill (who founded
the Denver Free Kindergarten Asso-
ciation in 1890). Suffragists who
were charter members of the WCD
included: Ione Hanna, Katharine Pat-
terson, Mary C. C. Bradford, Ellis
Meredith, Minnie J. Reynolds, Ella
Adams, Eliza Routt, Harriett Scott
Saxton, and Helen Marsh Wixson.
Public officeholders included:
Amelia Eddy, Thalia P. Rhoads, Minerva C. Welch, and Ione T. Hanna,
all of whom served on the Board of
Control of the State Industrial School
for Girls; Susan Ashley, Frances K.
Thatcher, and Laura P. Coleman,
who served on the Board of Lady
Managers of the World's Fair from
1891 to 1895; Helen Wixson, who
was assistant librarian from 1894 to
1896; and Dr. Minnie C. T. Love,
Sarah Platt Decker, Dr. Eleanor
Lawney, Nettie E. Caspar, Ella S.
Williams, and Anna G. Williams, all
of whom served at various times
from 1893 to 1915 on the Board of
Charities and Corrections. Nonchar-
ter members of the WCD who held
public office prior to 1900 were:
Angenette J. Peavey (state superintendent of public instruction, 1893–
95); Louise L. Arkins and Sarah
O'Bryan (Board of Control, State In-
dustrial School for Girls); and Dora
E. Reynolds, Louise Arkins, Anna
Cochran, and Luna Thatcher (Board
of the State Home for Dependent
Children. See *Officials of Denver and
Colorado, 1858–1933* (Denver: The
Denver Museum, 1934).

In 1896 there were 14 single
women in the NSWC among a total
membership of 163. Of this 14, no
occupation is listed in the DCD for 7
women; 5 were employed in business; and 2 were educators. By 1918

membership had stabilized at 125,
including 3 single women (NSWC
yearbook, 1917–18). All of these
NSWC members lived in the area
first known as Highlands before it
was annexed by the City of Denver.
As indicated in the DCD, the majority of these NSWC clubwomen in
1918 were the wives of white collar
or professional men.

46
Mary Louise Sinton, "A History of
the Woman's Club of Denver, 1894–
1915" (M.A. thesis, University of
Denver, 1980), 24.

47
Nancy F. Cott, *The Bonds of Womanhood: "Women's Sphere" in New England, 1780–1835* (New Haven: Yale
University Press, 1977), 194.

48
In this way, a Miss Fee of the TASC
retained her nonresidence status
(TASC minutes, 1910–24).

49
MLC resolution, October 4, 1921.

50
Millicent Van Riper, "Book Presenta-
tion of the Denver Fortnightly Club"
(Denver, November 17, 1959),
WH108, DPL.

51
Ashley, "A Very Brief Chronicle," 14.

52
WCD yearbook, 1908–9; NSWC yearbook, 1913–16.

53
Harriet Campbell, "There Were Gi-
ants in Those Irreclaimable Days"
(Denver, 1937), 5, WH108, DPL.

54
WCD yearbook, 1895–96. In this issue of the *News*, Mary C. C. Bradford, Ellis Meredith, Angenette Peavey, Ione Hanna, and Sarah Decker

gave their views on municipal reform, manual training courses, gambling, and the duties of clubwomen on reform and philanthropic work.

55
Grover Cleveland, "Woman's Mission and Woman's Clubs," *The Ladies Home Journal,* May 1905, 3.

56
Ibid., 3–4.

57
"Buchtel Again Vilifies the Women of His State," undated newspaper article in Martha A. Bushnell Conine scrapbook, 1896–1910, DPL.

58
DFC minutes, 1885–86. DFC members on the library committee were Ella Denison, Lucy Scott, and a Mrs. Mitchell.

59
Preiss, *The Colorado Federation,* 33.

60
Rocky Mountain News, April 21, 1895; *Denver Times,* October 22, 1899; Dorsett, *The Queen City,* 111; NSWC yearbook, 1897–98; WCD yearbook, 1900–1901.

61
Yearbooks of the WCD, the TASC, the NSWC, the MLC, and the RTC all show contributions for these institutions in one form or another. The Old Ladies' Home, in particular, has been a favorite project of the clubs, many of which have furnished rooms at the home and supplied magazine subscriptions.

62
Rocky Mountain News, October 24, 1898; *Denver Times,* October 22, 1899.

63
Duane A. Smith, *Mesa Verde National Park: Shadows of the Centuries* (Lawrence: University Press of Kansas,

1988), 42–54; Runnette, "In a Changing World," 39.

The Progressive Era

1
Dorsett, *The Queen City,* 154.

2
DFC yearbooks, 1900–1904.

3
MLC minutes, 1903–8.

4
RTC yearbooks, 1900–1914.

5
TASC yearbooks, 1900–1914.

6
Coleman, "The Turn of the Century," 8.

7
WCD yearbooks, 1900–1914.

8
NSWC yearbooks, 1900–1914.

9
Member clubs paid dues to the CFWC and the GFWC which, in turn, provided speakers, the exchange of ideas and methods through a newsletter and state meetings and visits, and the ability to mobilize large numbers of women for a particular cause or piece of legislation.

10
TASC minutes, 1910–24.

11
Preiss, *The Colorado Federation,* 34.

12
Ibid., 35.

13
Ibid., 17–18.

14
Campbell, "There Were Giants," 8. Besides those women mentioned in Chapter 2, Katherine Craig continued the clubwomen's domination of the state superintendency of public instruction. She held this position from 1904 to 1906, 1906 to 1908, and 1920 to 1922 (Papers of Katherine Craig).

15
NSWC yearbooks, 1902–12.

16
Ibid. The home, now called Argyle Park Square, is located at 4115 West Thirty-eighth Avenue in Denver (see *Rocky Mountain News*, July 12, 1987).

17
Collette and Fish, comps., *History of the Woman's Club*, 25.

18
Ibid.

19
Coleman, "The Turn of the Century," 20.

20
Campbell, "There Were Giants," 1.

21
DFC and WCD yearbooks. Other reforms in health and welfare supported by the Denver clubs as a whole included the Workshop for the Adult Blind; an eight-hour day for miners, laundry workers, and working women; factory inspections; free state employment bureaus; the establishment of a "School for the Feeble-Minded"; and a mothers' compensation act (Preiss, *The Colorado Federation*, 22).

22
DFC, MLC, TASC, WCD, and NSWC yearbooks. Taussig served on the Board of Control of the State Industrial School for Girls (see Campbell, "There Were Giants").

23
NSWC yearbooks, 1913–16.

24
Benjamin Lindsey and George Creel to Ellis Meredith, October 16, 1915.

25
Robert G. Athearn, *The Coloradans* (Albuquerque: University of New Mexico Press, 1976), 222. See also Smith, *Mesa Verde National Park*.

26
Ashley, "A Very Brief Chronicle," 30.

27
TASC minutes, 1910–24.

28
WCD yearbook, 1909–10.

The World War I Years

1
DFC, MLC, RTC, TASC, WCD, and NSWC yearbooks, 1914–20.

2
Ashley, "A Very Brief Chronicle," 25.

3
John Higham, *Strangers in the Land: Patterns of American Nativism, 1860–1925* (New Brunswick, N.J.: Rutgers University Press, 1955), 205.

4
Dorsett, *The Queen City*, 181.

5
Ashley, "A Very Brief Chronicle," 16.

6
A random survey of women in federated clubs in Denver shows that 20 percent also belonged to patriotic organizations and other groups that extolled their longtime ties to the American past. These include the Colonial Dames, the Daughters of the American Revolution, and the Daughters of the Confederacy.

7
DCD, 1914. Members of the Colorado Traveling Library Commission were WCD members Annie G. Whitmore, Fannie M. D. Galloway, and Katherine J. Wright. Members of the State Home for Dependent Children were Sarah Curtis, Margaret P. Campbell, and Dora E. Reynolds. The State Industrial School for Girls members were Louise Arkins, Mrs. G. W. Gano, and Ellen Van Kleeck. Of this list, only Curtis and Gano were not members of one of the six Denver federated clubs.

8
WCD yearbook, 1918–19.

9
Ashley, "A Very Brief Chronicle," 16.

10
NSWC yearbooks, 1910–12.

11
Bain, History and Chronology of the Colorado Federation, 43.

12
WCD and NSWC yearbooks, 1914–20; Denver Times, January 21, 1903; and Mary L. Parks, "Early Denver Resident Dies," The Denver Post, February 20, 1941.

13
Blair, The Clubwoman as Feminist, 118.

14
James, ed., Notable American Women, 452.

15
James H. Baker, ed., History of Colorado, vol. 3 (Denver: Linderman Co., Inc., 1927), 1002.

16
Ibid.

17
Rocky Mountain News, October 4, 1918.

18
Rocky Mountain News, May 9, 1919.

19
Ashley, "A Very Brief Chronicle," 14.

20
Ibid., 15.

21
RTC minutes, November 22, 1918.

22
Collett and Fish, comps., History of the Woman's Club, 29.

23
NSWC yearbook, 1918–19.

24
The Denver Post, May 13, 1917. Clubwomen on the women's council included: RTC members Virginia Shafroth (also of the MLC), Katherine M. Dines, Alberta Iliff, and Helen Miller (also of the MLC); MLC members Margaret Campbell (WCD and DFC), Eva LeFevre, Frances Belford, Leonora Bosworth, and Sara Taylor Arneill; WCD members Katherine Hosmer, Gertrude Vaille, Mary Grant, Fannie Galloway, and Martha Parriott; and NSWC members Mary McCue, Alice Crosby, and Lela Starr.

25
Rocky Mountain News, March 14, 1918.

26
Rocky Mountain News, January 30, 1918.

27
Rocky Mountain News, February 2, 1919.

28
WCD yearbook, 1914–15, and NSWC yearbook, 1915–16.

29
Mary E. Hiatt, "Fortieth Anniversary of the Twenty-Second Avenue Study

Club," October 18, 1933.

30
The Denver Post, April 15, 1918.

31
Campbell, "There Were Giants," 10.

32
The Denver Post, July 10, 1923; *Denver Times,* July 10, 1923.

33
Rocky Mountain News, April 21, 1919.

34
Rocky Mountain News, March 24, 1918; *The Denver Post,* March 28, 1917.

35
WCD yearbook, 1919–20.

36
TASC minutes, February 6, 1918, and WCD yearbook, 1918–19.

37
NSWC yearbook, 1917–18; TASC minutes, April 9, 1919; WCD yearbook, 1918–19; Ashley, "A Very Brief Chronicle," 16.

Postwar Years and Depression

1
Athearn, *The Coloradans,* 242.

2
While the four smaller Denver clubs maintained their stability in total numbers, over one third of their current members had joined in the 1920s, and between 40 and 75 percent had joined within the previous twenty years. During the 1920s, DFC membership remained constant at 34; MLC at 29; and the RTC's membership grew from 32 in 1920 to 39 in 1927. The TASC began with 34 members in 1920; by 1924, the number was down to 26, with four of the eight losses due to death.

The club then grew to 30 members and held steady. Since club minutes and yearbooks note the year members joined, it is possible to determine the length of membership.

Many prominent club leaders died during the 1920s. Within the DFC, there were eight deaths, among them Ione Hanna (a member from 1881 to 1924), Jennie Baker (member 1889–1926), Anna Wolcott Vaile (member 1898–1928), Margaret Patterson Campbell (member 1912–29), and Ella McNeil (member 1889–1925).

The MLC lost Margaret Campbell (1912–29; president 1925–26), Helen Ring Robinson (1902–23; president 1911–12), Helen Marsh Wixson (1893–1925; president 1903–4), Dr. Mary Barker Bates (1889–1924; president 1900–1901), and Mrs. Ethelbert Ward (1912–27; president 1922–23).

The RTC, led from the beginning by Alice Polk Hill, lost her to death in 1921, followed by three more club members in the 1920s. The TASC, which had had only four deaths in the first ten years of its existence, had eight in the 1920s. Two, Emma Ruggles and Adelle Kling, were charter members. However, the most drastic change in this club came in 1924 when Nettie C. Caspar stepped down from the presidency after having held that position since 1894.

As was the case before the 1920s, the WCD experienced a fluctuation in membership during the decade. Between 1920 and 1922, membership dropped from 271 to 254; between 1922 and 1928, membership rose to 387. Deaths of past WCD presidents included Margaret Campbell (1894–1929), Elizabeth Byers (1894–1920), Alice Polk Hill (1894–1921), Helen Marsh Wixson (1894–1925), Ella Vincent (1894–1920), and Ella McNeil (1894–1925). In addition, several members who had been prominent leaders in the early years had moved on to positions with the CFWC and were no longer active in the WCD. Nettie Jacobson was federation president from 1918 to 1920, Jessie Munroe from 1924 to 1925 (she died during her term in office), and Nora Wright from 1926 to 1928 (Bain, *History and Chronology of the Colorado Federation*, 42–60). Six WCD charter members still belonged by 1929.

The last club, the NSWC, had sixteen deaths during the 1920s, leaving only eight charter members by 1929. At the beginning of the decade membership totaled 107; by 1925, it had increased to 236; but by the end of the decade, membership had again dropped to 208.

The older members in all the clubs were replaced with women who would become the leaders in the 1930s and later. New members in the DFC included: Carla D. Swan (Mrs. Henry), daughter of charter member Ella Denison, and Mrs. William Iliff. New members of the MLC who would become presidents were Obie P. Dunklee (1933–34), Alice B. Humphreys (1935–36), and Mary F. Spalding (1936–37). In the TASC, Zimmie Rupp (1939–42), Harriet E. Slusser (1933–35), and Dora Kenworthy (1936–37) joined the club in the 1920s and later became presidents (DFC, MLC, and TASC yearbooks, 1920–40).

3
Bain, *History and Chronology of the Colorado Federation*, 42.

4
Robert Goldberg, *Hooded Empire: The Ku Klux Klan in Colorado* (Urbana: University of Illinois Press, 1981), 28.

5
Ibid., 88–89.

6
Ibid.

7
The Denver Post, December 8, 1924; WCD yearbook, 1920–22, 1922–24.

8
The Denver Post, December 8, 1924.

9
The Denver Post, November 24, 1924, 29; Goldberg, *Hooded Empire*, 110.

10
The Denver Post, May 13, 1942.

11
Goldberg, *Hooded Empire*, 89.

12
The Denver Post, August 9, 1925; Goldberg, *Hooded Empire*, 110.

13
The Denver Post, November 24, 1925; Goldberg, *Hooded Empire*, 110.

14
Goldberg, *Hooded Empire*, 16.

15
Athearn, *The Coloradans*, 247–48.

16
The rebellion in the women's Klan between the factions of Dr. Love and Laurena Senter, however, received some mention in the newspaper. With club records unavailable for viewing at the WCD at this time, this writer can only surmise the reaction of other clubwomen to the Klan involvement of Love and Senter. It is also difficult to determine what other, if any, clubwomen were involved in the Klan. Two lists at the Colorado Historical Society indicating members and dues-paying members of the Klan are not identical. Care must be used in examining them and drawing conclusions regarding who actually belonged to this organization. Archival material of the Gano Senter family has been submitted to the Western History Department of the Denver Public Library and is unavailable to researchers at this time. However, it is possible to conclude that the women's involvement in the Klan did not *ap-*

pear to seriously weaken the positions of Senter and Love in the WCD.

Love lived in Denver until her death in 1942. As a charter member of the WCD, she became an honorary life member in 1932 (WCD yearbook, 1932–35). In her obituary, she was praised for her humanitarian service (*The Denver Post*, May 13, 1942). Laurena Senter was elected president of the WCD (1936–38) and later became an honorary life member of the club (WCD yearbooks, 1936–43). Thus, their involvement did not tarnish Love's and Senter's standing in the WCD. Perhaps they, too, like Stapleton, only used the Klan to advance their own causes and later denounced the bigotry and methods of the organization.

17
DFC and MLC minutes, 1926–30; WCD and NSWC yearbooks, 1910–24; TASC minutes, 1910–24.

18
Bain, *History and Chronology of the Colorado Federation*, 61.

19
MLC minutes, December 1, 1930; RTC minutes, January 26, 1934.

20
Hiatt, "Fortieth Anniversary of the Twenty-Second Avenue Study Club," October 18, 1933. Anyone who was at least willing to work could be a member in 1895–96. In 1900 the club limited membership to forty-five, the number of women who could be comfortably accommodated in private homes. A long waiting list of two to three years was common in the early years.

21
TASC, MLC, and WCD yearbooks.

22
The Denver Post, May 5, 1934. A note found in Ballantine's pocket-

book said, "I cannot face another operation. I am not as brave as I used to be."

23
MLC minutes, March 19, 1934.

24
NSWC yearbooks, 1930–39.

25
WCD yearbook, 1938–39.

26
MLC minutes, October 3, 1932.

27
TASC minutes, 1924–40.

28
WCD yearbook, 1934–35.

29
Ibid.

30
NSWC yearbook, 1934–35.

World War II Years

1
The Denver Post, June 8, 1914.

2
Florence Rena Sabin Papers, Colorado Historical Society, Denver.

3
MLC yearbooks, 1940–46; RTC yearbooks, 1940–46.

4
Mary E. Hiatt, "History of the Twenty-Second Avenue Study Club, 1941–42," MS965, Colorado Historical Society, Denver.

5
NSWC yearbooks, 1940–46.

6
Lucille Kling became the club's second historian in 1943 and shows

strong opinions in her histories. In 1944 she blasted a condescending newspaper article entitled "Developing Personality" which urged women to "read the newspaper, including the editorials daily." She wrote: "Surprising! What do they think we do with it, nothing but decorate the pantry shelves? Come gentlemen! wake up! the day is long past when feminine readers were interested in nothing but the Women's Page and the Monday bargains!" (Lucille Kling, "History of the Twenty-Second Avenue Study Club, 1943–44" [hereinafter TASC history, 1943–44]).

7
Lucille Kling, "History of the Twenty-Second Avenue Study Club, 1944–45" (hereinafter TASC history, 1944–45), MS965, Colorado Historical Society.

8
Kling, TASC history, 1943–44.

9
Ibid.

10
Kling, TASC history, 1944–45.

11
Bain, *History and Chronology of the Colorado Federation*, 81.

12
NSWC yearbook, 1942–43.

13
WCD yearbooks, 1941–43.

14
WCD yearbook, 1941–42.

15
Bain, *History and Chronology of the Colorado Federation*, 82.

16
Kling, TASC history, 1943–44; Kling, TASC history, 1944–45.

17
Mildred McClellan Melville, "History of the American Women's Voluntary Services, 1941–1944" (Denver, 1944), Colorado Historical Society. See also Kling, TASC history, 1943–44.

18
Kling, TASC history, 1943–44.

19
Kling, TASC history, 1944–45.

20
Dorothy Fallon, "History of the Twenty-Second Avenue Study Club, 1945–1946" (hereinafter TASC history, 1945-46), MS965, Colorado Historical Society.

21
Lyle W. Dorsett, *The Queen City*, 238–39.

22
Ibid., 239.

23
WCD yearbook, 1942–43.

24
Kling, TASC history, 1944–45; Fallon, TASC history, 1945–46.

25
Kling, TASC history, 1943–44.

26
Interview with Zimmie Rupp, TASC, Denver, Colorado, October 15, 1986.

27
Bain, *History and Chronology of the Colorado Federation*, 82.

28
Kathryn Jo Davis, *Red Cross Remembers* (Colorado History Museum exhibit, May 4–September 7, 1987, Denver, Colorado).

29
NSWC yearbooks, 1942–44.

30
Kling, TASC history, 1943–44.

31
Ibid.

32
Fallon, TASC history, 1945–46.

33
Rocky Mountain News, March 14, 1940.

34
MLC yearbooks, 1940–49.

35
MLC minutes, October 1, 1945.

36
RTC yearbooks, 1940–49. This brought the total number of deaths for this club to thirty-one (in fifty-six years). Attendance at each meeting continued to be over 65 percent.

37
The loss of these four members resulted in the club's having only five members with twenty years or more standing and nineteen with ten or less. This marked a definite change from earlier years when most of the clubs had been members for over one or two decades (TASC yearbooks, 1940–49).

38
Ibid.

39
Rocky Mountain News, January 6, 1944.

40
WCD yearbooks, 1940–44.

Lynda F. Dickson

Lifting as We Climb

African-American Women's Clubs
of Denver, 1890–1925

About the author
Lynda F. Dickson is an
associate professor of sociol-
ogy at the University of
Colorado at Colorado
Springs. Her teaching and
research areas include the
sociology of family, poverty,
and race and ethnic relations.
She has been published in
*Free Inquiry in Creative
Sociology* and in *The Journal of
Black Studies,* and has written
an article on the Negro
Women's Club Home
Association in *Black Women
in America* (1993).

THE PERIOD OF RECONSTRUCTION found black Americans generally optimistic about their future as full-fledged citizens—a condition, they believed, that would come about through the economic, political, and educational elevation of the race. For most of them, economic advancement—manifest through hard work, sobriety, and acquisition of wealth and property—was the key to full assimilation. Those who had already gained some degree of economic security stressed the attainment of political and civil rights. Yet, in spite of efforts in these areas, increasing racial prejudice and discrimination, especially in the South, was such that by the late nineteenth century, what few gains had been made had all but disappeared, and the 1890s marked the beginning of a period of decline in the status of black Americans which would continue through the 1920s.

By 1910 virtually all of the southern states had disenfranchised black citizens through amendments to state constitutions. In the North, while black political and civil rights still existed on paper, overt prejudice and discrimination was rapidly becoming the norm, so that by the early 1900s northern public opinion concerning African-Americans mirrored that of the South on questions of racial inferiority, denial of the franchise, and the justification for white domination.

Recognition of increasing racism and the very real social problems that were rapidly becoming a part of the black experience had a tremendous impact on African-American thinking during this period. As early as the 1890s black optimism concerning full participation in mainstream society was gradually replaced by a sense of realism: Perhaps the focus should first be placed upon *preparation* for full participation. A change of tactics was called for. Although economic advancement continued to be emphasized, political and civil rights and full assimilation—while remaining long-range goals—were replaced by the belief that blacks must first accumulate wealth and develop the virtues of cleanliness, thrift, and high moral character. The assumption was that once wealth and morality were achieved—and largely through their own efforts—blacks would gain the respect of whites and thus be "worthy" of full citizenship. Thus, self-help and racial solidarity became the dominant defensive philosophy.

In spite of the conflicts between "radicals" and conservatives within the black community, the major theme in African-American thought on the race question from the last decade of the nineteenth century through the 1920s remained clear: The progress of the race could be achieved only through the united effort of the race itself. The emphasis on self-help and racial solidarity as defense reactions to white hostility and exclusion was manifest in all areas. Religious and educational institutions, business and professional associations, and cultural societies such as literary and study clubs—all adhered to this ideology. Especially prevalent during the 1890–25 period was the enthusiastic development of benevolent, social reform, and social welfare organizations within black urban communities. According to W. E. B. DuBois,[1] these organizations represented "the efforts of the better classes of Negroes to rescue and uplift the unfortunate"; and a recent scholar claims that no single force better illustrated these efforts among blacks than the activities of women's clubs.[2]

DURING the late 1880s and early 1890s, Denver experienced rapid growth, and increasing numbers of blacks, along with other racial groups, came to the city in the hope of improving their lot. By 1890 a distinct black community had emerged.[3] Because of the (albeit limited) opportunities that existed—largely through providing services to this community—a prosperous, if small, middle class was soon established. It is from this class that the leaders of the club movement came. Many were recent arrivals from larger cities who had been exposed to and recognized the potential of women's clubs in helping the less fortunate within the race.

Elizabeth Piper Ensley was one such person. She had studied abroad during the 1870s, and upon returning to the United States had established a circulating library in Boston, where she became a public schoolteacher. In 1882 she married Horwell N. Ensley and moved to the District of Columbia where they served on the faculty at Howard University. They later moved to Mississippi where Elizabeth Ensley taught at Acorn University.[4] In the early 1890s the Ensleys moved to Denver, and Elizabeth quickly became active in club work. One of the founding members of the Woman's League of Denver, which was organized by black women around 1894, she served as Denver's correspondent to the *Woman's Era*, the official journal of the National Association of Colored Women.

In the June 9, 1894, issue of the *Woman's Era*, Ensley described the active role that black women had played in an election earlier that spring—the first time women in Colorado had been allowed to vote. She noted the "special part . . . colored women have taken in the election. Most of them have done admirable work in the interest of the Republican party. They also formed clubs on their own and heroically helped their brothers to elect a representative to the legislature, although the majority of those brothers voted against women's enfranchisement." This was not the first time that Denver's black women had organized to press for political and civil rights. A *Rocky Mountain News* article of February 11, 1885, offers evidence that at least one organization, the Colored Ladies Legal Rights Association, engaged in direct political action of the kind that informed post–Civil War strategies to gain civil rights. It was partly responsible, in fact, for a state civil rights bill, which provided penalties for denying equal rights in places of public accommodation.[5]

In 1904 Ensley founded the Colorado Association of Colored Women's Clubs—an idea that had begun to form as early as 1896, for Ida DePriest, another early club mover, had mentioned the possibility of such an organization to the National Association during that year.[6] DePriest was also a member of the Woman's League of Denver, serving as corresponding secretary in 1895–96.[7] She appears to have been most often linked with political activities, working through the Colored Women's Republican Club of Denver. This club, according to the *Denver Times*, had accomplished "more telling work in the last two campaigns than any other colored organization in the state."[8]

While they lasted, these late-nineteenth-century clubs represented broader, more politically active interests than those that were established after the turn of the century. Even their names serve to indicate this shift in interests—from the Colored Ladies Legal Rights Association, the Colored Women's Republican Club, and the Woman's League of Denver to the Pond Lily Art Club, the Taka Art and Literary Club, the Book Lovers Club, and the

Carnation Art Club. Corresponding to broader ideological changes occurring among black intellectuals during the late nineteenth century, agitation by Denver's black clubwomen for equal political, economic, and social rights was gradually replaced with an emphasis on *preparation* for equal rights. Self-help, self-improvement, and racial unity became the dominant themes of the day, and the work of Denver clubwomen was no exception.

The new emphasis on self-improvement may also help explain why the most prevalent types of clubs came to be those directed toward the study of art, literature, music, and needlework. The Woman's League, one of the clubs formed prior to 1900, had complained to the National Association of Women's Clubs in 1895 that the work of the league had been "crippled" by the loss of women who were insecure about their capabilities. Women who joined clubs devoted to art or needlework no doubt perceived them as less personally threatening than membership in a politically active club and could further justify their decisions by the prevalent ideology of self-improvement. This is not to suggest, however, that black clubwomen were unconcerned with the broader issues affecting the race as a whole—especially the goal of helping the less fortunate. In fact, the newer clubs used their skills in music, art, and needlework as major sources of fundraising for that purpose. On the state level, for example, the clubs founded and supported the Colored Orphanage and Old Folks Home in Pueblo, a project that received continuing assistance through donations of money, food, and clothing.[9]

At least twenty-two federated clubs in Denver were organized between the years 1900 and 1925. Many of them lasted only a short time, then disbanded; others, as membership declined, merged with the stronger clubs. A few managed to withstand the test of time, and some still exist. Four currently existing clubs which were organized in the first quarter of the century are the focus of this study: the Pond Lily Art and Literary Club, the Taka Art Club, the Carnation Art Club, and the Self-Improvement Club.[10] All are members of city and state federations and are members of the National Association of Colored Women. In addition, they were—and still are—part of an association that established a day nursery in 1916, the maintenance of which was a major factor in the success and survival of the clubs for more than seventy-five years.

Of the four clubs, the Pond Lily Art and Literary Club is the oldest. It was organized in the late summer of 1901 by Augustavia Young Stewart, who was then sixteen years old.[11] According to the club's historian, Young had become incensed over a local newspaper article that had made derogatory statements about black women. She decided to form a club composed of young women who could, through thought, word, and deed, help dispel negative stereotypes about women of color. She called upon other young women who were not yet out of high school, and they held their first meeting in City Park. During that meeting, they noticed the lilies floating in the pond and decided to call the club Pond Lily.

The immediate goal of the new organization was self-improvement. The members decided that they would develop their talents so that whether they were playing the piano in public, reciting their favorite poems, reading a paper, or reviewing a book, it would be done in a way that would help create a better opinion of colored people.

The club was officially organized in 1902, and its first president, Florence Walden, served in that capacity until 1908. The object of the club—very much in line with the prevailing conservative philosophy of racial betterment through moral uplift—was to "bring the women of Denver into communication for closer acquaintance, mutual helpfulness, and the promotion of higher social and moral conditions."[12] According to the State Federation of Women's Clubs, Pond Lily became a member in 1906.

Two of the other clubs under study were organized in 1903. The first, the Taka Art and Literary Club, was founded by Minnie Norman and Mary Chapman to promote mutual helpfulness.[13] The second, the Carnation Art, Literary, and Charity Club, was founded by Savilla Burnett to bring "Negro women closer together in friendship and love" and to make the community a better place in which to live. The object of the Carnation Club, according to its constitution, was to learn "how to educate our hands by doing needlework to beautify homes, broaden our minds, and bring us closer together in friendship and love."[14]

The last club under study, the Self-Improvement Club, was organized in 1906 to foster "improvement of self along all lines of literary, art, charitable and social activities." It had as its ultimate aim "to maintain a home for young women who might come to Denver and who lacked proper protection."[15] The Self-Improvement Club is credited as being the originator of the idea for the Girls Home and Day Nursery, organized by the Negro Woman's Club Association in 1916.

FORMAL STRUCTURE and rigid adherence to rules and regulations were important during the early life of the clubs. The number of officers to be elected, as well as the specific duties of each office, were clearly stated, as were the number of meetings to be held per month and the activities to be carried out within each meeting. The club year ran from October to June, ending with the state association conventions, usually held during the first or second week in June. During this time, Taka Art met once a week on Wednesdays, the first Wednesday of the month being literary day while all others were devoted to art work. Carnation Art held its weekly meetings on Fridays, with the second Friday of the month being literary day. The Pond Lily and Self-Improvement clubs met on every other Thursday.

Club members felt they could work best by limiting the size of their membership: The Pond Lily and Taka Art clubs held their membership to twenty; the Carnation Art and Self-Improvement clubs had a ceiling of thirty members. Further, all clubs worked through departments or committees, including ways and means, reciprocity, domestic science, rescue, and programing, with members either volunteering or being appointed to serve.

Requirements of members—including the wearing of club regalia, the number of pieces of artwork expected, the amount of dues, how often members were expected to act as hostess for meetings, and how they were to conduct themselves within and outside of club meetings—were clearly stated in the bylaws, as well as the fines to be imposed for failure to fulfill these requirements. Judging from the number of fines imposed—which ranged from two cents for not being prepared with a quotation during roll call, to twenty-five cents for not attending a city federation meeting, to one dollar for not having a finished piece of art work for the state association conference—clubs rigidly followed these bylaws.

Expulsion from the clubs could result from misconduct or overbearing behavior by club members or from spreading club news to outsiders. During a 1917 meeting of the Taka Art Club, for example, its president noted that "someone told her that some member of the club was talking club news to other than club members," and she would find out who it was if it was the last thing she did.[16]

During the early years, club meetings were held at members' homes, usually rotating alphabetically. But judging from the frequency with which certain names are mentioned, it appears that those members who had larger homes were called upon more often to act as hostess. In any event, after the Negro Woman's Club Home was established in 1916, clubs began holding all their meetings there.

The agenda for meetings was similar for all clubs. The president would call the meeting to order, and the club's chaplain would offer some form of devotional such as the Lord's Prayer or a scripture reading. Roll call generally followed, and members were required to respond with a biblical quotation which, at least in the case of Taka Art, they had to recall from memory to avoid a two-cent fine. For all meetings other than those on literary day, a work period of at least an hour ensued in which members worked on art pieces. In some cases, especially in the early years, an art teacher came to the club and worked with the women until they had developed the skills necessary to act as teachers themselves. After the work period, members concluded old business, took up new business, and paid dues (ten cents a week initially) before adjourning. After adjournment, the hostess would serve light refreshments.

In addition to similarities in purpose, structure, and format, these clubs had similar requirements for membership. Candidates had to have "willing hands," a "desire to help others," and an eagerness "to do something for the race—especially the children."[17] Furthermore, considering that a major aim of the clubs was to uplift the image of black womanhood, it is not surprising that the most common requirement was that the applicant have "high moral character." Aside from these expectations of membership, however, little may be found in the clubs' minute books and ledgers that paint an accurate portrait of Denver's black clubwomen—who they were, how they lived, and what motivated them to join. Nevertheless, a few remaining members who joined clubs prior to 1925—along with others no longer living whose stories could be reconstructed from the public record and interviews—shed some light on the lives of these women.

Florence Moore, one of the oldest surviving federated women in Denver when interviewed in 1982, had been an active member of the Carnation Art Club since 1917, and had rarely missed a meeting. Born in 1890 in San Marcos, Texas, she had come to Denver at the age of twenty-six to be with her husband, who was a railroad electrician, and had immediately joined the Carnation Club. She recalled that while most of the other members were married, they were also older than she, and while some of them were day workers, most were homemakers. Although she herself was not employed when she joined, her husband died in 1927 and she had worked from that time on. When asked about her educational background and that of other members, Moore indicated that she had completed eight years of school and that the other members had completed about the same number of years.[18]

Ora Harvey of the Pond Lily Art Club had similar recollections about other club members. Born in 1895 in Fort Smith, Arkansas, Harvey had spent her early years in Kansas City. She moved to Denver in 1920 and became a member of Pond Lily in 1925. At that time she was thirty years old, and she recalled that the ages of other members varied. Although single when she joined, she soon married a man who, like Moore's husband, worked for the railroad. Most of the other members were married, and about half of them had children. She was employed soon after moving to Denver by a "very rich white woman" as a live-in housekeeper and earned the then high salary of one hundred dollars per month. Most of the other members, she recalled, were also employed—some as domestics but others as hairdressers and seamstresses, and one as a schoolteacher. Harvey had a sixth-grade education when she joined

Pond Lily; most of the others, she recalled, had at least a high school diploma.[19]

Reverend Susie Whitman was also a federated woman during the 1920s, but was no longer active. She had joined the Taka Art Club shortly after moving to Denver in 1927, and at the time she was thirty-three years old, married, and had one child. Other members, she recalled, were "mostly younger" than she but were also married and had children. Though she was not employed then, she recalled that other members were ministers' wives, teachers, or in some cases domestics. Reverend Whitman had completed four years of college, while most of the other members had achieved a high school education.[20]

All of these early club members indicated that their co-members were "Christian women" interested in "uplift work." A common church affiliation, however, was not the major determinant for membership in a given club, for members belonged to various churches. In fact, neither common church membership, mutual acquaintances, nor close residential proximity had much to do with a woman's decision to join a club. Florence Moore, for example, had only recently moved to Denver and knew no one there. But her husband, who played cards with Ada Webster (then president of the Carnation Art Club) mentioned to Webster that his wife was moving to Denver. Webster introduced Moore's name to the club, and she readily consented to become a member.[21] Ora Harvey had a similar experience with the Pond Lily Club. Her husband, who had lived in Denver for some time before she moved to the city, belonged to a card club with Corinne Lowry, who was a Pond Lily member. Harvey's husband introduced the two, and Lowry submitted her name to the club. Both Florence Moore and Ora Harvey indicated that they had never regretted their initial decision. As Harvey pointed out, she was a member of Pond Lily for over fifty years, and stated, "I'll die a Pond Lily."

For other members, however, it was necessary to go through a period of trial and error with clubs before they found the one that best suited them. Reverend Whitman indicated that she first joined Pond Lily but soon found that "the same person who invited me to join ended up working against me," so she left after only a few weeks. Later, Rev. Whitman joined the

Taka Art Club, which she believed was "the cream of the crop."[22]

Gertie Ross, another member of the Taka Art Club, was particularly active in the early years. Born in Kansas in 1879, she moved with her family to Denver in 1881. She was an honor graduate of East High School, attended the Western Conservatory of Music, and did postgraduate work in New York. Returning to Denver, she taught music classes and was organist and musical director for the Shorter A.M.E. Church for twenty years. Ross was the first black woman employed by the United States Mint in Denver, where she served as a weigher.[23] In 1910 she married George Ross, an attorney, who also published the *Denver Star*, one of the earliest black newspapers in Denver.

Gertie Ross was a member of Taka Art club from at least 1913 until her death in 1961, during which time she devoted her almost limitless energies to club work. Others described her as a "tireless worker" who had "a memory like an elephant" and who was always interested in furthering her education. According to Reverend Whitman, Ross knew something about everything and could "out-think anybody with a college degree"—in fact, she worked on her degree while a club member. Her interest in education no doubt contributed to her initiating the idea for an education fund, established in 1920 by the State Association of Colored Women's Clubs.[24] This fund, managed by a board of directors, gave scholarships to worthy young women, and Ross worked with this board throughout her career as a federated clubwoman.

While Ross's work with the state association, for which she served as president in 1918, is certainly worth mentioning, her continuous involvement with the local club provides the clearest picture of a truly committed clubwoman. Judging from Taka's minutes, Ross was the force that held the club together and kept the members aware of parliamentary etiquette—of which she had considerable knowledge—and continually reminded members when they strayed from proper procedures. She not only contributed to writing and revising Taka's constitution and by-laws, but would explain these in such a way that the members could easily understand. The club's minutes suggest that she was a hard taskmaster: "Mrs. Ross" states one entry, "suggested a remedy for members' talking during the meeting." Another reads, "Mrs. Ross gave a splendid talk on conduct of members."[25] That her colleagues may have been ambivalent about Ross's "suggestions" for the improvement of the functioning of the club is indicated in her receiving the dubious honor of election as "club critic" in 1916.

Ross also kept before the club any charity cases in the community which had been brought to her attention. She encouraged the club to form a committee to survey the community to determine how many colored families needed help, and to present this information to influential community leaders for their assistance.[26]

Perhaps because of her husband's contacts through the *Denver Star*, Ross was wellinformed on most issues and activities in the black community. In 1916, for example, she reported on a woman who wanted to adopt an eight-year-old girl, and asked club members to let her know if they knew of such a child. She was especially aware of the need for clubwomen to participate in civil rights issues. When black community leaders organized to protest the showing of D. W. Griffith's *Birth of a Nation* in 1916, she strongly encouraged the club to send two representatives. She was also part of a committee appointed by the club to investigate a report that a Denver Dry Goods Company discriminated against its colored employees by forcing them to use specially designated restrooms.[27]

Finally, Ross kept the club informed of current works in the black intellectual community. During a program in 1915, she read from Booker T. Washington's "Exceptional Men" and, in the following year, read and reviewed the article "Are We Making Good?" by Margaret Washington. While there is less information on most of the other early clubwomen, Ross was not an exceptional case. Two other Taka members, Lillian Bondurant and Helen Gatewood, also provided direction to the club.

Bondurant was born and raised in Harrodsburg, Kentucky. In 1907, at twenty-five, she moved to Denver and in 1912 married Samuel Bondurant, who owned and operated the Bondurant Cleaners.[28] According to Taka's minutes, Bondurant visited the club in December 1914, but her name was not presented as an applicant until the next October. She was officially voted into the club on October 13, 1915.[29] From that time until her death in 1974 she worked tirelessly for the club. She was especially active in the Negro Woman's Club Home Association, established in 1916, chairing its board of directors for many years.

Helen Gatewood spent much of her adult life in Pueblo where she was active in both club and church work. When she moved to Denver in the early teens, she first focused on working with her church, New Hope Baptist, where she organized several youth groups. Her interest in young people carried over into her club work, for when she joined Taka in 1917, she devoted much of her time to working with the club home's day nursery and dormitory for young girls.[30] She served as the home's president for seven years. By the time of her death in 1945, she had donated a car to the home as well as the property at Twenty-eighth and Humboldt.[31]

One last example of a committed clubwoman is Ada Webster of the Carnation Art Club. Webster was serving as secretary to the club when it was asked to cooperate with other clubs in establishing a club home in 1916. Members were so split over the idea that all of the officers and most of the members resigned. Webster stayed and became president of the club. She encouraged the few remaining members to join the other clubs, and under her leadership the club sponsored a chitterling dinner to raise its share of the money needed to open the home.[32]

For the most part, then, early clubwomen were generally married and had children, were high school graduates, and considered themselves Christian women. Well over half were employed as elocutionists, musicians, seamstresses, milliners, domestics, and laundresses. One major indication that many of the early members were employed (and in domestic and laundry work, at that) is the fact that meetings for all clubs were held on weekdays (domestics and laundresses rarely had Saturdays off).[33] But whether employed or not, all of the members felt a sense of obligation toward uplift efforts within their clubs, for they were actively involved in helping the less fortunate within the community. While some of the women may be considered outstanding exceptions, a major requirement of the early clubs was a commitment to hard work. Judging from the number of resignations from members, those who were not willing to contribute the amount of time and energy—not to mention money—needed by the clubs did not continue as members.

INTERESTS AND ACTIVITIES of the clubs varied so much that it would be difficult to place them into neat categories. However, they focused on efforts to improve members' skills in arts and crafts, including music and literary and intellectual development; helping the poor and needy individually and through more formalized "giving," such as contributing to the Red Cross; assisting the community's attempt to combat discrimination; working with children to encourage higher health and educational standards; and sponsoring mothers' meetings, girls' clubs, and fundraising activities. All these activities required a tremendous amount of teamwork not only within but between clubs. To be a "federated woman" meant more than actively participating in one's own club; it meant living up to expectations of assisting other clubs in larger efforts and causes. In this, two types of activities were paramount: (1) assistance for the poor and needy, and (2) the most important example of collective action between clubs, the Negro Woman's Club Home.

A primary objective of the clubs was to give direct assistance to cases of individual need that came to the attention of clubwomen. When members heard of someone who was impoverished, sick, or in trouble, they would report it to the club and the group would decide whether to provide outright assistance; to refer the case either to the benevolent, charity, or rescue committees for investigation; or, in a few instances, to decide against providing help.

The Taka Art Club's minutes offer concrete examples of such help. In 1915, for example, one woman was given a pair of shoes and another a ton of coal—both of which cost the club $6.20. Further, states the minutes, "Mrs. Clay's little boy needs shoes" ($2.00 was allocated) and "Mrs. Jackson needs assistance" (her rent was paid for a month, and she was given a sack of flour).[34] In 1916 the club allotted $1.00 for a prescription for a sick woman; $5.00 to purchase artificial limbs for a disabled man; $1.50 to help a woman secure a railroad ticket; and $2.00 to assist a destitute family.[35] In many instances, clothing, medicine, or food replaced direct cash contributions; in others, money was the only medium possible, as in 1920, when Taka Art members gave $5.00 to secure bond to release a woman from jail. Also during that year, the Taka Art Club received a letter from a mother in Colorado Springs whose son had recently been sentenced to the state prison in Cañon City. The club donated $10.00 to assist in his appeal.[36]

In spite of all this, Taka members did not give blindly. In fact one member, Georgia Contee, suggested in 1919 that Taka spend more time finding out whether the unfortunate "really needed help" before deciding to give it.[37] Occasionally the relief committee visited a sick individual or family and reported that no help was needed. Other factors influenced the decision in 1921, however, for when Helen Gatewood presented the case of a woman with two children whose parents were about to put her out, the motion to pay part of her rent was denied.[38]

Not only did the club provide assistance to what it considered deserving individuals, it also made regular contributions to the YWCA either in the form of money or materials. When Lillian Bondurant reported to the club on YMCA needs, members donated six sheets costing $3.00. The club also made regular contributions to the Red Cross and the Federated Charities, an organization for which the club raised $303 in 1921.[39] After the Community Chest was established in 1922, Taka members pledged regularly and paid off their contributions in weekly installments.

The Carnation Art Club provided similar kinds of individual and collective assistance, including carrying coal and wood to poor families, paying rent, assisting girls from the South to buy railroad tickets so that they could return home, giving shoes and clothing to needy families, and donating baskets of food at holidays like Thanksgiving and Christmas. Carnation members also established a "milk fund" for underprivileged children and made regular contributions to both the YMCA and the YWCA, Shorter, Zion, and Central Baptist churches, the Colored Blind Home, the Community Chest, and the Lincoln Orphanage in Pueblo.[40]

As is no doubt evident from this charity work, clubs needed to raise a considerable amount of money. Thus, a great deal of time and effort went into fundraising through various activities.

These included card parties, bake sales, rummage sales, home-cooked dinners, concerts, poetry readings, and plays. Fundraising efforts were usually conducted under the auspices of the ways and means committee, but often members were asked to donate directly to a specific cause. Either these donations came out of pocket or the more creative (or less financially able) would hold their own entertainments (such as box suppers or card parties) and turn the proceeds over to the club. In 1918 Georgia Contee raised over thirty dollars through an entertainment benefit, and the Takas were so pleased that they sent the news to the *Denver Star*.[41] Other fundraisers given by the Taka Art Club included an "entertainment" in 1914, a "guessing contest" in 1916, and a "Japanese entertainment" in 1918. They featured a play, *Wages of Sin*, in 1919 and hosted a Martha Washington tea party in 1920. The Carnation Art Club had similar types of fundraisers as well as an annual Clown Dance, a chitterling dinner, and, in 1918, an "Uncle Sambo and Aunt Dinah" entertainment.[42]

In order to encourage attendance at these events, the clubs would often give a small prize, such as a dress pattern or a middy waist, for either the first person in the door or the person bringing the most guests. All this, in any case, required a tremendous amount of cooperation among the members. While no doubt true of most club endeavors, it was particularly true in the fundraising: The members worked as a team, and each member gave according to her ability, or her means. When the clubs sponsored a bake sale, for example, it was rare that clubwomen donated whole products, such as a cake or a pie. Instead, they usually gave ingredients—sugar, eggs, or flour—and those members who were unable to contribute would volunteer to do the actual baking.[43]

Club membership thus involved a commitment to—and active participation in—a wide range of activities, including assisting the poor. While certain members may have shown more commitment than others, the successful functioning of the clubs called for considerable cooperation, and this extended well beyond the individual clubs. In fact, the most salient example of cooperative teamwork between clubs was the establishment and maintenance of the Negro Woman's Club Home.

THE IDEA of a club home for which several clubs would be responsible was first suggested by Georgia Contee of the Self-Improvement Club. Contee had recognized the need for a place where colored girls coming to Denver might stay. Since this was too ambitious an undertaking for one group, the Self-Improvement Club invited the presidents of the other clubs in Denver to consider supporting such a home. While the most logical organization to consider the proposition would have been the city federation, the only recorded action, according to Taka's minutes, was taken by the Self-Improvement Club.[44] The most reasonable explanation for this less-than-unanimous action is that some of the clubs in the city federation objected or were unwilling to take on such a responsibility, so the name of the city federation could not be placed on the home. In any event, seven clubs responded to the challenge—Taka Art, Pond Lily, Carnation Art, Self-Improvement, Progressive Art, Sojourner Truth, and Twentieth Century—and these became known as the Negro Woman's Club Home Association.

The decision to become a part of the Club Home Association was no doubt difficult for many of the clubs. In fact, as has been stated, the Carnation Art Club split over the issue to the point that all its officers resigned with the exception of Ada Webster, the club's secretary. Webster, along with six remaining members, kept the club alive. Under her leadership, Carnation joined the Club Home Association, raised the necessary funds for its share in getting the home started by throwing a large chitterling dinner, and ultimately became the second club to pay off its share of stock in the home—no small feat given the club's small membership.

During late 1915 and early 1916, the association met regularly to make plans for the home. Each club submitted an idea for "the ideal club home," and Taka's suggestion was typical:

> The home should take up all lines of charity, rescue, nursery, [and] employment. . . . A committee [should be established] to look into the matter of educational rights, . . . a committee to look after Colored children who have been arrested to see that they are given a fair trial—[and] . . . anything else that might help humanity.[45]

The Taka Art Club also suggested a fundraising campaign, which began with a mass meeting held in July at Shorter Chapel.[46] Six months later, on December 16, 1916, the clubs moved into a modern, two-story brick structure at 2357 Clarkson Street. The home, which consisted of eight rooms, was incorporated for five thousand dollars with each club buying equal shares of stock, at ten dollars per share. The aim of the new home was the maintenance of a dormitory, while the lower floor housed the nursery.[47]

It is understandable that virtually all surviving club members, when asked "What was the most important activity for you in your club?" responded without hesitation—"The running of the nursery." For not only was considerable time and effort devoted to raising money to purchase shares of stock, but the clubs were also responsible for soliciting sustaining members— either individuals or groups who would pay a sustaining fee of twelve dollars—or associate members, who paid six dollars per year toward the maintenance of the home.

Not only was such a commitment ambitious, but it is pertinent that the association—consisting of seven clubs—itself became a federated club, and joined the city, state, and national associations. This meant that members in the individual clubs were required to pay weekly club dues—and the club in turn paid city, state, and national dues—but because the club was also part of the association, it also had to contribute to the city, state, and national dues required of the association! When these dues were added to the numerous collections taken up during the meetings for one purpose or another regarding the home— combined with the collections made for charity cases, contributions to the YWCA, and other organizations to which the clubs were expected to contribute—it is little wonder why one irate member of Carnation Art Club would suggest, "Why not raise the club dues rather than nickel-and-dimeing us to death?"[48] It is also understandable why all of the Denver clubs did not wholeheartedly embrace the idea of becoming part of the Club Home Association.

In addition to raising money for the home, the clubs also contributed whatever the home currently needed, ranging from dishes and other utensils, milk, bread, and even clothing for the children in the nursery, to the purchase of sheeting for the exterior of the building, screens for the windows, and rakes for the yard. Yet perhaps more important than any of these contributions was the amount of time spent in the home. Ora Harvey of the Pond Lily Club recalled that she "changed many a diaper" and "cooked many a meal" for the home. Other members recalled working toward keeping the facility clean and running smoothly. Some of the members devoted seemingly unlimited energies toward the home. Lillian Bondurant, who variously served as chair of the board of directors for the association, was known to make valuable suggestions for ways to cut corners, such as buying meat wholesale or contacting Oliver T. Jackson, head of the black agricultural colony at Dearfield, to solicit fresh vegetables for the home.[49]

Given the time and energy it took to get the home established and running smoothly, it is not surprising that the board of directors ran a tight ship. Every aspect of the home's functioning was taken seriously—from establishing the rules for the dormitory and nursery to hiring, and later firing, a yard man. The secretary maintained meticulous accounts of each transaction occurring in the home, and every action taken by the board was initiated by parliamentary motion, including insurance payments and the purchase of meat and staples.

By far the most important staff member in the home was the matron. She was responsible for endless tasks, especially involving the running of the dormitory. Young working women could rent a room in the dormitory for $1.25 per week including kitchen privileges (the price was increased to $1.50 in 1920 and $2.00 in 1924).[50]

The "inmates"—as the residents were called—were governed by strict rules upheld by the matron: They were not allowed to bring furniture, boxes, trunks, or pictures into the home; lights were to be out by 10:30 P.M.; all washing and ironing were to be done in the laundry room during specified days and hours, at a rate of twenty-five cents per person; and electric irons were prohibited in the building. Girls were responsible for making their own beds and keeping their portion of the room tidy, and they were "absolutely prohibited" from lounging on vacant beds. To use the kitchen, they had to make arrangements with the matron, and they were at all times to use the dining room for lunch hour, using club dishes, and leave the kitchen and dining room as found.[51]

The rules of the home clearly indicated the clubwomen's desire to instill proper training and morality in the girls. Specific requirements for washing dishes ("Must use pan instead of sink; must use soap when washing dishes"), personal grooming ("Arrangements of toilet, including the straightening of hair, must be done in one's room"), or entertainment of "company" ("Must use the parlor and matron must be present") were rigidly upheld.

The matron was responsible for assigning beds to the girls, as well as bath times. Arrangements had to be made with her in order to use gas, water, and heater. She was also required to evict any person who was found destroying property or not following the rules. But the matron's duties did not end with the dormitory maintenance. She also opened the building at 7:00 A.M. and closed it at 6:00 P.M.; she was responsible for all cases of emergency; and she itemized weekly reports of transactions in the home (accounts for dormitory and nursery were to be kept separately). She prepared the menus, collected fees for entertainments (or socials) in the home, and was responsible for the behavior of the children, including teaching them proper table manners. As if these duties were not enough, she was also admonished to "make the home comfortable and at all times take the place of mother for the girls entering the home."[52] For all of these responsibilities, the matron's salary was forty dollars per month in 1920.[53]

In 1919 clubwomen of the association took up the question of allowing married women to stay in the dormitory. This issue was taken back to the individual clubs for a vote. While Taka approved the idea, most of the clubs did not, for the June 13, 1919, minutes of the association show that the board requested married women to move. In 1920 it recommended that the association rescind the earlier action concerning who could stay in the dormitory, but the motion lost.

Both the nursery and dormitory proved successful, and in 1921 the association's report to the State Board of Charities and Corrections indicated that the home had four paid officers—one man and three women—including a second matron. The nursery cared for thirty children, and the dormitory housed nine girls.[54] In addition to the dormitory and nursery, the home allowed various community organizations to rent its facilities for entertainments—stipulating that these could not be card parties, dancing parties, or political meetings. The women's clubs began holding their weekly meetings in the home, paying the nominal fee of fifty cents per meeting, while rent charged to other organizations was three dollars. In this way the association contributed to the home's income and became a community center in the process.

In spite of what was clearly an enormous undertaking to maintain the home, the association also sponsored yearly fundraisers such as Harvest Home (a yearly bazaar) and a charity ball. Although members of the association occasionally pointed out that as Christian women they should put on some form of entertainment other than a charity ball, this was nevertheless continued for a number of years. Another method of raising funds for the home was through raffles. In 1922, for example, a lace work was given to the association by a "a white man" and was raffled off at ten cents a chance.[55]

The association's concern with raising funds for the home led to soliciting help from the Denver Federation of Charities. When this organization became defunct in 1922, the clubs joined the Community Chest, where as members their responsibilities actually increased: They were required to participate in fundraising drives, maintain additional records on the home, and publicize the Community Chest by providing reports of anything novel or newsworthy that occurred there.

In spite of the small stipend received from the Community Chest, the association remained primarily responsible for maintaining the home and in making improvements. In 1923 the board noted that, since the Community Chest would "give us nothing for a new building, and realizing if we expect to improve our home it must be through our own efforts, the Board recommends that the Association establish a building fund."[56] Each of the seven clubs in the association was to put in one hundred dollars per year for two years, or until enough money was raised. On October 2, 1926, the Taka Art Club made its second installment of twenty-five dollars toward the building fund, and in 1927, as a result of such donations, a sun parlor was built on the home at a cost of $2,700 cash.[57]

In addition to a continuing concern about money, the association maintained an interest in all of the details surrounding the functioning of the home. When the work of the yard man was found to be unsatisfactory, the board paid his monthly salary and dismissed him; when it learned that the first matron had been performing part of the second matron's work, it saw that she was paid an additional $5.33; when it learned that the mothers of children in the nursery were not as involved as they might be, it established "mothers meetings."[58]

Another major activity, beginning in 1921, was the establishment of a health clinic in the home. The association had earlier recognized the need to relieve the congestion at the clinic located at Twenty-sixth and Lawrence, as well as the inconvenience this clinic posed to mothers who had to take their children such a distance. But it also knew that it must have the cooperation of the community if the clinic were to be successful. Thus, members of the board visited doctors in the area to determine whether or not they would be willing to cooperate, while other members visited the homes of mothers in the area to be assured that they would in fact use the clinic. After getting their support, the association pursued the idea, and the clinic was officially opened in 1922.[59]

In other respects, too, as community needs changed, so did the home. When the YWCA sponsored the building of a dormitory for black women during the early 1920s, the association found less use for its own dormitory. At the same time, however, there was a growing need to expand the nursery. Thus, the dormitory was eliminated, and the association thereafter devoted most of its energies toward maintaining the nursery.

In addition to the seemingly endless tasks associated with the maintenance of the nursery, dormitory, and clinic, the association was, of course, also a federated club. This meant that, like other clubs, it was required to participate actively in city, state, and national functions as well as contribute to various fundraisers, help with individual cases of charity, and generally assist in other community uplift efforts. In terms of assisting needy individuals, in 1921 alone the association gave assistance to a needy Denver family; investigated the well-being of a girl living in Denver whose concerned mother had called to inquire about her from Chicago; sent a large quantity of clothing to the poor and needy in Tulsa; and, after hearing of the sad plight of a girl in the Crittendon Home who was in dire need of shoes and clothing, readily provided these items.[60]

Monetary support was an ongoing necessity for the association. In 1922, when one of the residents in the home became ill, the association decided that since clubwomen were essentially providing her lodging, the clubs should also give fifty cents per week for her food. As the condition of the young woman worsened, the association discussed placing her in the hospital, and she was referred to the charity committee. The young woman's sister eventually arrived to help care for her, and the clubs were asked to support the two women.[61]

The association was also interested in cases of discrimination in Denver. In one instance, the chair of the house committee reported the arrest of one of the girls in the home, stating that the whole affair was "deplorable, in as much as the girl was innocent of the charge [and] was humiliated in having to ride in the patrol car and being roughly handled by the officers."[62] In 1923 a member of the board recommended that a letter be written to Governor Sweet commending him on his "splendid attitude" on the segregation of public schools in Denver. Also during 1923, a board member was appointed to investigate the report that the community lodging house had denied service to colored people. In cases where little could be done about discrimination, the association nevertheless expressed its concern, as in its report of a girl about to be hanged in Washington, D.C. Members were asked to pray for the commutation of her sentence, and the president urged all who could to attend a prayer meeting to be held in the home.[63]

Each activity of the association—whether it was participation in Community Chest drives, assisting the YWCA, sponsoring fundraisers for the Club Home, or hosting Christmas parties for the children in the nursery—required sincere commitment from each club. Their contributions ranged from buying stock, soliciting sustaining members, and making donations to the home, to devoting time and energy toward the home's maintenance.

As in most instances in which members of an organization must spend considerable time together, occasional conflicts arose. These stemmed from personality clashes as well as club differences. In 1920, for example, an oversight on the part of the secretary led to a reprimand by the association's president, Isabelle Stewart, who called on the other gathered members to ask what should be done with a secretary who neglected her duties. "That's what's wrong with the Association now," she said, suggesting that members were leaving too many things undone. Then, moved by anger, Stewart blamed the association for omitting her name from a newspaper story about the Club Home and ended by verbally submitting her resignation. "My superiors won't insult me," she said, taking her seat, "my inferiors can't insult me."[64] This precipitated a later argument between the president and the chair of the social committee, Sarah Abernathy, on the question of who initiated the idea for the Club Home. Stewart produced and read from what she claimed was the 1914 yearbook of the Self-Improvement Club, which proved, she stated, that Georgia Contee was in fact the originator. Abernathy questioned the authenticity of the book, and an argument ensued during which Abernathy was told to "shut up" so the issue could be settled. The association members eventually credited Contee with the idea for the home, and Abernathy resigned, as did the secretary who had been accused of neglecting her duties.[65]

In spite of these differences, clubwomen managed to stick together rather than let personal grudges and club allegiances destroy what they had worked so hard to accomplish. Three of the seven clubs eventually disbanded, and in that way left the association, but the remaining clubs—Pond Lily, Self-Improvement, Carnation, and Taka Art—still comprise the Negro Woman's Club Home Association. The name of the nursery was changed to George Washington Carver Day Nursery in 1946 and is now housed in a modern building in Denver.

CLEARLY, black women's clubs in Denver fulfilled important functions for the community, but equally important were the functions fulfilled for the women themselves. Sophrinisbe Breckenridge, in *Women in the Twentieth Century*, points out that women's organizations emerging during the early twentieth century served as places where members "could find refreshment, recreation, or culture, cultivate some intellectual or social interest or accomplish some public-spirited good."[66] In the matter of accomplishing "public-spirited good," according to some historians and sociologists, women's clubs were more effective in social, civic, and educational reform than were men's. In *Black Metropolis,* St. Claire Drake and Horace Cayton explain this, in the case of black women's activities, as a result of the fact that women were trusted by the black community because they were perceived as less likely to capitalize from "race issues."[67]

Another explanation offered for both black and white women's greater success at reform efforts is that such efforts represented, on a broader scale, issues addressed by women within their own communities. Cheryl Townsend-Gilkes argues that black women's work "represents extensions of their concerns and problems faced as wives and mothers within the community."[68] Not only did club activities in Denver serve as expressions of personal concerns, but there was a sense of personal satisfaction derived from self-improvement activities, providing assistance to the less fortunate, and especially in maintaining the nursery and dormitory.[69]

Quite apart from the general women's club movement, however, black clubwomen were actively involved in both instilling and maintaining the values of racial uplift. This was apparent in virtually all of their activities, including the effort toward improving the members' skills in the arts and crafts as well as homemaking, encouraging a sense of race pride by keeping before both the members and the community the "outstanding" achievements of members of the race, and, perhaps most importantly, serving as a positive example of what could be accomplished through united effort.

White women's clubs emerged as a reaction to the dominant nineteenth-century perception that women could not work together, could not accomplish much, and were not interested in anything beyond the home and family. But there is a difference between the effort of women to prove themselves in the face of patronizing male attitudes and the need of black women to assert the value of both their sex and their race in the face of white racism. White women's organizations represented the "best women" working toward their own improvement, and their efforts at helping the less fortunate were such that they could distance themselves and thus not become personally involved. Black women's organizational efforts, especially those directed at helping others, represented the relatively few "better women" who had a personal stake in "lifting as we climb." Because of this, black clubwomen shared the need to improve their negative image not only through providing positive role models, but through working with young black women as well as those who were less fortunate than themselves. Given the recognition that the task before them was an enormous one, it appears that a major function of club participation for its members was primarily to provide a support system which could eventually reinforce members' belief that the task was, in fact, possible.

1
W. E. B. DuBois, Some Efforts of American Negroes for Their Own Social Betterment (Atlanta University Publications, No. 3, 1898), 5; Inabel Burns Lindsay, "The Participation of Negroes in the Establishment of Welfare Services, 1865–1900" (Ph.D. diss., University of Pittsburgh, 1952), 121–32.

2
While these clubs played a significant role within their communities, the general neglect or underestimation of their activities and achievements has been the rule rather than the exception. Furthermore, the exceptions have focused on the nation's major organization, the National Association of Colored Women, established in 1895, which maintained careful records of its activities. Considerably less is known about local club movements that formed during the same period and that later affiliated with the National Association. While initial clues may be found in early correspondence between the national, state, and city associations, the task remains to provide a thorough investigation of club activities on the local level and to place them in the social and ideological context in which they functioned.

The 1980s witnessed a number of attempts to fulfill this task, with several works on black women's club activities in Indianapolis, San Francisco, Cincinnati, Washington, D.C., and Kansas. See, for example, Earline Rae Ferguson, "The Woman's Improvement Club of Indianapolis: Black Women Pioneers in Tuberculosis Work, 1903–1938," Indiana Magazine of History 3 (1988): 237–61; Marilyn Dell Brady, "Organizing Afro-American Girls' Clubs in Kansas in the 1920's," Frontiers 9 (1987): 69–73; Marilyn Dell Brady, "Kansas Federation of Colored Women's Clubs, 1900–1930," Kansas History 9 (1986): 19–30; Andrea Tuttle Kornbluh, "Woman's City Club: A Pioneer in

Race Relations," QueenCity Heritage 44 (1986): 21–38; Sharon Harley, "Beyond the Classroom: Organization Lives of Black Female Educators in the District of Columbia, 1890–1930," Journal of Negro Education 51 (1982): 254–65.

Undoubtedly one of the reasons for the renewed interest in the history of black women's club activities is the apparent reemergence of self-help advocates within black communities. It is also interesting to note the similarities in perceived problems within black communities—unemployment, youth crime, unstable families, and conflicts between black men and women.

3
According to Gerda Lerner, there are three preconditions to club development among black women during the period 1890 to 1925: sizable black population, educated women with leisure time (to provide the leadership), and unmet needs of the black poor. See Gerda Lerner, Black Women in White America (New York: Random House, 1973), 436–67.

4
"Milestones of the State Association of Colored Women's Clubs," undated scrapbook, Western History Department, Denver Public Library.

5
Group thesis, "Contributions by Blacks to Social Welfare History in the Early West" (M.A. thesis, University of Denver, 1974), 116.

6
National Association of Colored Women's Clubs, Inc., A History of the Club Movement among the Colored Women of the United States of America (Washington, D.C.: National Association of Colored Women's Clubs, Inc., 1902), 83.

7
Ibid.

8
Denver Times, March 28, 1901.

9
State Federation of Colored Women's Clubs (hereinafter CWC) minutes, 1904–20, 115; CWC ledger, 1913, 33 (in Western History Department, Denver Public Library).

10
The research method for examining these clubs was as follows: The author contacted historians from each club and gained permission to examine all available materials, which included minute books (by far the best source of information), ledgers, scrapbooks, announcements of activities sponsored by the clubs, and numerous miscellaneous items. The condition of these materials depended upon a variety of factors, including the conscientiousness of the historians and the writing skill of the early secretaries and historians. Much of the information on the period in question has either been destroyed or misplaced over the years; thus, the available sources are limited. In addition, the same type of information is not available for all clubs. Yet from the materials which are consistent for all clubs it appears that the clubs were so similar in purpose, structure, format, and activity that it is possible to provide a "picture," so to speak, of the typical club. In addition to examining available materials, the author interviewed the oldest living member of each club. These interviews were helpful in clarifying questions that emerged in reviewing written materials.

11
James T. Atkins Collection, Box 48, File 2164, Colorado Historical Society, Denver.

12
Pond Lily Art Club constitution and bylaws, in possession of Ora V. Harvey, Denver, Colorado.

13
Interview with Dorothy Reaves, April 2, 1981.

14
Carnation Art Club constitution and bylaws, in possession of Florence Moore, Denver, Colorado

15
Brochure for the State Federation of Colored Women's Clubs, 1928, Western History Department, Denver Public Library. This brochure contains brief sketches of clubwomen and clubs in the state federation.

16
Taka minutes, February 7, 1917.

17
Interviews with Florence Moore (Carnation), February 1982; Susie Rose Whitman (Taka), February 1982; and Ora Harvey (Pond Lily), January 1982.

18
Interview with Florence Moore.

19
Interview with Ora Harvey.

20
Interview with Rev. Susie Whitman.

21
Interview with Florence Moore.

22
Interview with Rev. Susie Whitman.

23
State Association minutes, 1904-1910.

24
Taka minutes, February 18, 1914.

25
Taka minutes, December 2, 1914, and February 7, 1917.

26
Taka minutes, December 1, 1915.

27
Taka minutes, December 1, 1915.

28
Biographical notes on Lillian Bondurant are included in papers held by Dorothy Reaves, Denver, Colorado.

29
Taka minutes, October 13, 1915. This point is made because most of the Taka information for later years refers to Bondurant as one of the earliest members. Some of the current members believed she was a charter member.

30
Taka minutes, February 17, 1917.

31
Notes maintained by Dorothy Reaves, Denver, Colorado.

32
Brief historical sketch of the Carnation Art Club.

33
However, as members of the Coterie Club (the one nonfederated club which the author examined that is not a part of this study) were quick to point out, theirs was the only club which always held meetings on Saturdays—clearly implying that there were no domestics or laundresses in the club. (Coterie Club minutes, 1916, 1918, 1920; interview with Coterie historian, Edith Hawkins, a Coterie member since 1916).

34
Taka minutes, May 12, February 4, and February 24, 1915.

35
Taka minutes, January 1, February 2, March 8, March 29, and July 19, 1916.

36
Taka minutes, March 12 and October 20, 1920.

37
Taka minutes, December 17, 1919.

38
Taka minutes, February 16, 1921.

39
Taka minutes, February 2, 1921.

40
Carnation Art Club, "Summary of Past Contributions," undated.

41
Taka minutes, September 1, 1918.

42
Carnation minutes, January 5, 1917, December 4, 1918.

43
Taka minutes, May 25, 1920.

44
Taka minutes, March 8, 1915.

45
Taka minutes, March 8, 1916.

46
Carnation minutes, July 14, 1916.

47
Negro Woman's Club Home brochure, 1924, in possession of Dorothy Reaves, Denver, Colorado.

48
Carnation minutes, December 3, 1918.

49
Minutes of the Negro Woman's Club Home Association (hereinafter NWCHA), October 5, 1920; minute book in possession of Dorothy Reaves, Denver, Colorado.

50
NWCHA minutes, June 1, 1920; 1924 brochure.

51
NWCHA minutes, June 1, 1919 ("Rules Governing Dormitory").

52
NWCHA minutes, July 1, September 2, 1919 ("Rules for Matron").

53
NWCHA minutes, February 2, 1920.

54
Annual report to the State Board of Charities and Corrections for the year ending June 20, 1921, in possession of Dorothy Reeves, Denver, Colorado.

55
NWCHA minutes, December 15, 1922.

56
Ibid., March 6, 1923.

57
NWCHA brochure, 1927.

58
NWCHA minutes, April 4, 1922.

59
Ibid., February 7, 1922.

60
Ibid., September 6, July 5, October 4, 1921.

61
Ibid., May 2, July 5, and October 3, 1922.

62
Ibid., October 4, 1921.

63
Ibid., October 5, 1920; March 6, 1923.

64
Ibid., January 6, 1920.

65
Ibid.

66
Sophrinisbe Breckenridge, Women in the Twentieth Century (New York: McGraw-Hill, 1933), 5.

67
St. Claire Drake and Horace R. Cayton, Black Metropolis (New York: Harcourt, Brace, 1945), 543.

68
Cheryl Townsend-Gilkes, "Holding Back the Ocean with a Broom: Black Women and Community Work," *The Black Woman*, ed. La Frances Rodgers-Rose (Beverly Hills, Calif.: Sage Publications, 1980).

69
When members were asked to identify their most important club activities, by far the most common response was the pride they felt in in participating in their club's contributions toward the nursery. In fact, their enthusiasm for this topic made it difficult to steer them away from the subject of the Club Home to other issues.

WOMEN'S CLUBS AND CLUB MEMBERS
(Mentioned in the Text)

Carnation Art Club

Burnett, Savilla
Moore, Florence
Webster, Ada*

Denver Fortnightly Club

Ashley, Susan Riley [Eli M.], vice president; president*
Baker, Jennie
Campbell, Harriet
Campbell, Margaret Patterson
Coleman, Carla Denison Swan [Albert J.]
Cooper, Jane O. [Job A.]
Craig, Katherine
Denison, Ella [Charles], founder; president*
Evans, Margaret Gray [John], president*
Hanna, Ione [John R.], secretary-treasurer; president*
Iliff, Mrs. William
Keely, Elizabeth
Kountze, Mary [Charles]*
McNeil, Ella [John L.]
Patterson, Katharine Grafton [Thomas M.]
Reynolds, Dora E. [A. E.]
Sabin, Florence R. (Dr.)
Scott, Lucy E. R. [George L.]*
Spalding, Elisabeth
Spalding, Lavinia [John F.]*
Spalding, Mrs. William
Spalding, Sara Griswold
Swan, Carla D. [Henry]
Vaile, Anna Wolcott [Joel F.]

Monday Literary Club

Arneill, Sara Taylor [James Rae]
Ballantine, Ida Winne [George W.]*
Bates, Mary Barker (Dr.)
Belford, Frances
Bennett, Julie R. [Horace W.]

*Charter member

Monday Literary Club *(Continued)*	Bingham, Ada* Bosworth, Leonora Snyder [Joab O.]* Campbell, Margaret Patterson Caspar, Nettie E. [Stanley M.] Dunklee, Obie P. [Edward V.] Dunklee, Mary E. [George F.] Ferris, Ermina D., president* Humphreys, Alice B. Kinney, Leila LeFevre, Eva F. [Owen] McAllister, Phoebe [Henry] McCrary, Sue, president Miller, Eva Miller, Helen Robinson, Helen Ring [Ewing] Shafroth, Virginia Morrison [John F.] Spalding, Mary F. Ward, Mrs. Ethelbert Wixson, Helen Marsh [Elmer A.]*

**North Side Woman's
Club**
	Chase, Mary [T. C.], president
	Conine, Martha A. B. [John], president*
	Cornwall, Amy [W. T.]
	Crosby, Alice [J. C.]
	Hilliard, Tida Z. [Benjamin C.]
	Irish, Sarah [E. M.]*
	Johnston, Millie C. [J. C.]*
	McCue, Mary [W. F.]
	Parks, Mary L. [James], president*
	Starr, Jeannette M.*
	Starr, Lela
	Turner, Mabel M. [Albert F.]
	Welles, Julia V. [A. M.]*
	Wheeler, Frances M. [Charles]*
	Wolff, Sarah A., founder and first vice
	    president*
	Wright, Harriet G. R. [Henry], pres-
	    ident*

Pond Lily Art and Literary Club	Harvey, Ora Lowry, Corinne Stewart, Augusta Young, founder* Walden, Florence* Whitman, Rev. Susie

Round Table Club	Bennett, Julie R. [Horace W.]
	Berger, Mrs. William
	Bonney, Mrs. J. W.*
	Brent (Miss)
	Dines, Katherine M. [Tyson]
	Ellis, Alverta [Miss], president
	Fisher, Mary F. [William G.]*
	Hill, Alice Polk, president*
	Iliff, Alberta
	Jacobson, Nettie C. [Charles H.]*
	McCrary, Sue T. [Napoleon]*
	McCrea, Florence [Harry], president
	Miller, Helen
	Sargent, Florence
	Seifried, Josephine [Frank], president*
	Shafroth, Virginia Morrison [John F.], president*
	Shaw, Mrs. Fred C., president
	Taussig, Marguerite
	Whiteman, El Frieda [W. J.], president*

Self-Improvement Club Contee, Georgia

Taka Art Club	Bondurant, Lillian
	Chapman, Mary
	Contee, Georgia
	Gatewood, Helen*
	Norman, Minnie
	Reaves, Dorothy
	Ross, Gertie
	Whitman, Rev. Susie

Twenty-Second Avenue Study Club	Bartlett, Alice H. [William J.]
	Caspar, Nettie E. [Stanley M.], president*
	Duling, Christine W. [David]
	Henry, Alice G. [Frederick T.]
	Hiatt, Louisa [R. J.]*
	Hiatt, Mary E.*
	Jeancon, Lionna F. [Jean Allard]
	Kenworthy, Dora [L. E.]
	Kling, Adelle E. [Orlando]*
	Kling, Lucille
	Ruggles, Emma [Almon]
	Rupp, Zimmie, president

Twenty-Second Avenue
Study Club *(Continued)*

Slusser, Harriet B. [C. R.]
Steidley, Jennie
Thomas, Edna B. [Frederick W.]
Weir, Minnie Lorena [Gilbert R.]
Weisser, Maude D. [William B.]

**Woman's Club of
Denver**

Adams, Ella [Alva]*
Arkins, Louise L. [John]
Ashley, Susan Riley [Eli M.]*
Bailey, Adelle [Dewey C.], president
Bingham, Ada*
Bradford, Mary C. C. [Edward T.]*
Brown, Mary L. [Junius F.]*
Byers, Elizabeth [William]*
Campbell, Margaret Patterson
    [Richard C.]*
Caspar, Nettie E. [Stanley M.]*
Chase, Mary [T. C.]
Cochran, Anna
Coleman, Laura P. [Robert J.]*
Conine, Martha A. B. [John M]*
Cooper, Jane O. [Job A.]*
Cornwall, Amy [W. T.]*
Coy, Helen P. [Nathan B.]*
Decker, Sarah (Sophia Chase) Platt,
    president*
Denison, Ella [Charles]*
Eddy, Amelia [Edward]*
Evans, Margaret Gray [John]*
Fish, Lisbeth [A. G.], president
Galloway, Fannie M. D. [W. K.],
    president
Grant, Mary [James B.]*
Grenfell, Helen
Hanna, Ione [John R.]*
Hawley, Antoinette Arnold [Theodore]
Hill, Alice Polk [William]*
Hill, Alice Hale [Nathaniel P.]*
Hosmer, Katherine [George E.]
Jeancon, Lionna F. [Jean Allard],
    president
Jorndt, Lucile [C. G.], president
Kountze, Mary E. [Charles B.]*
Lawney, Eleanor (Dr.)*

Woman's Club of
Denver *(Continued)*

LeFevre, Eva [Owen E.]*
Love, Minnie C. T. (Dr.) [Charles G.]*
MacPherson, Honora [John],president
McCrary, Sue T. [Napoleon B.]*
McCrea, Florence [Harry F.]*
McNeil, Ella [John L.]*
Meredith, Ellis
Munroe, Jessie H. [Herbert M.],
   president
O'Bryan, Sarah
Parriott, Martha
Patterson, Katharine Grafton
   [Thomas M.]*
Peavey, Angenette J. [A. J.]*
Reynolds, Dora E. [A. E.]*
Reynolds, Minnie J.*
Rhoads, Thalia P. [A. G.]*
Robinson, Helen Ring [Ewing]
Routt, Eliza F. [John L.]*
Saxton, Harriett Scott
Scott, Lucy E. R. [George L.]*
Senter, Laurena [Gano], president
Shafroth, Virginia Morrison [John F.]
Thatcher, Frances K. [J. A.]*
Thatcher, Luna [M. D.]
Vaile, Anna Wolcott [Joel F.]
Vaille, Gertrude [Joel F.]
Vincent, Ella [B. T.]*
Warren, Elisabeth Iliff [Henry W.]*
Welch, Minerva C.
Welles, Julia V. [A. M.]*
Whiteman, El Frieda [Wilberforce J.]
Whitmore, Annie G. [James D.]*
Williams, Anna G.
Williams, Ella S.
Wixson, Helen Marsh [Elmer A.]*
Wright, Harriet G. R. [Henry]*
Wright, Katherine J. [W. D.]
Wright, Nora [J. P.]

INDEX

INDEX OF CLUBWOMEN

Adams, Ella, 60
Arkins, Louise L., 60, 63
Arneill, Sara Taylor, 11, 50, 57, 63
Ashley, Susan Riley, 18, 30, 41, 56, 60

Baker, Jennie, 34, 64
Bailey, Adelle, 19
Bain, Jeannette, 56
Ballantine, Ida Winne, 41
Bancroft, Mary Caroline, 56
Bartlett, Alice H., 41, 50
Bates, Mary Barker, 10, 57, 64
Belford, Frances, 63
Bennett, Julie R., 11, 32
Berger, Mrs. William, 32
Bingham, Ada, 10
Bondurant, Lillian, 80–81, 87, 97
Bosworth, Leonora Snyder, 63
Bradford, Mary C. C., 30, 41, 60
Burnett, Savilla, 74–75
Byers, Elizabeth, 7, 60, 64

Campbell, Harriet, 34, 60
Campbell, Margaret Patterson, 11, 55, 58, 60, 63, 64
Caspar, Nettie E., 10, 13, 24, 41, 57, 60, 64
Chapman, Mary, 74
Chase, Mary, 15
Cochran, Anna, 60
Coleman, Carla Swan, 57
Coleman, Laura P., 60
Conine, Martha A. B., 15
Contee, Georgia, 83, 84, 85, 92
Cooper, Jane O., 20
Cornwall, Amy, 31
Craig, Katherine, 62
Crosby, Alice, 63
Curtis, Sarah, 63

Decker, Sarah Platt, 13, 14–15, 16, 25, 59, 60

Denison, Ella, 8–9, 49, 56, 61, 65
Dines, Katherine M., 63
Duling, Christine W., 41, 50, 59
Dunklee, Mary E., 10–11, 57
Dunklee, Obie P., 50, 65

Eddy, Amelia, 60
Ellis, Alverta, 58
Ensley, Elizabeth Piper, 55, 71–72
Evans, Anne, 30
Evans, Margaret Gray, 8, 9, 56

Fallon, Dorothy, 67
Fee, Ella, 59
Ferris, Ermina D., 9
Fish, Lisbeth, 35
Fisher, Mary F., 32
Francis, Mary, 41

Galloway, Fannie M. D., 63
Gano, Mrs. G. W., 63
Gatewood, Helen, 80, 81, 83
Grant, Mary, 63
Grenfell, Helen, 41

Hanna, Ione T., 8, 9, 12, 25, 60, 64
Harding, Minnie L., 25
Harvey, Ora, 77–78, 87, 96
Hawley, Antoinette Arnold, 31
Henry, Alice G., 41, 50
Hiatt, Louisa, 59
Hiatt, Mary E., 41, 50, 59
Hill, Alice Hale, 60
Hill, Alice Polk, 11, 17, 58, 59, 64
Hilliard, Tida Z., 51
Hosmer, Katherine, 63
Humphreys, Alice B., 41, 65

Iliff, Alberta, 63
Iliff, Mrs. William, 65
Irish, Sarah, 15

Jacobson, Nettie C., 31, 65
Jeancon, Lionna F., 50–51
Johnston, Millie C., 15
Jorndt, Lucile, 41

Keely, Elizabeth, 34–35
Kenworthy, Dora, 65
Kinney, Leila, 50
Kling, Adelle E., 50, 64
Kling, Lucille, 46, 66–67
Kountze, Mary E., 56

Lawney, Eleanor, 60
LeFevre, Eva F., 11, 50, 57, 63
Love, Minnie C. T., 38–39, 60, 65–66
Lowry, Corinne, 78

McAllister, Phoebe, 11, 50, 58
McCrary, Sue T., 50
McCrea, Florence, 59
McCue, Mary, 63
McNeil, Ella, 28, 64
MacPherson, Honora, 41
Meredith, Ellis, 27, 30, 60
Miller, Emma, 59
Miller, Eva, 50
Miller, Helen, 63
Moore, Florence, 77, 78, 96
Munroe, Jessie H., 65

Norman, Minnie, 74

O'Bryan, Sarah, 60

Parks, Mary L., 15, 31, 51
Parriott, Martha, 63
Patterson, Katharine Grafton, 58, 60
Peavey, Angenette J., 60
Preiss, Neata, 25, 56

Reaves, Dorothy, 96, 97, 98
Reynolds, Dora E., 20, 60, 63
Reynolds, Minnie J., 20, 6
Rhoads, Thalia P., 60

Robinson, Helen Ring, 11, 32, 34, 57, 64
Ross, Gertie, 79–80
Routt, Eliza F., 60
Ruggles, Emma, 64
Runnette, Mabel Mann, 57
Rupp, Zimmie, 48, 52, 56, 65

Sabin, Florence R., 4, 41, 44
Sargent, Florence, 50
Saxton, Harriett Scott, 60
Scott, Lucy E. R., 61
Seifried, Josephine, 59
Senter, Laurena, 38, 39, 65–66
Shafroth, Virginia Morrison, 11, 50, 58, 63
Shaw, Mrs. Fred C., 59
Shuler, Anne, 25
Sinton, Mary Louise, 60
Slusser, Harriet E., 65
Spalding, Elisabeth, 11, 17, 58
Spalding, Lavinia, 41, 56
Spalding, Mary F., 65
Spalding, Sara Griswold, 58
Spalding, Mrs. William, 17
Starr, Jeannette M., 15
Starr, Lela, 63
Steidley, Jennie, 47
Stewart, Augustavia Young, 74
Stewart, Isabelle, 92
Swan, Carla D., 65

Taussig, Marguerite, 32, 62
Thatcher, Frances K., 60
Thatcher, Luna, 60
Tyler, Louise, 12

Vaile, Anna Wolcott, 9, 25–26, 64
Vaille, Gertrude, 30, 63
Van Kleeck, Ellen, 63
Van Riper, Millicent, 60
Vincent, Ella, 64

Walden, Florence, 74
Ward, Mrs. Ethelbert, 64

Walker, Caroline, 22
Warren, Elizabeth Iliff, 60
Webster, Ada, 78, 81, 85
Weir, Minnie Lorena, 51
Weisser, Maude D., 13, 41, 59
Welch, Minerva C., 60
Welles, Julia V., 20, 24
Wheeler, Frances M., 15
Whiteman, El Frieda, 41
Whitman, Susie Rose, 78–79, 96
Whitmore, Annie G., 20, 63

Williams, Anna G., 60
Williams, Ella S., 60
Wixson, Helen Marsh, 10, 57,
   60, 64
Wolcott, Anna. *See* Vaile, Anna
   Wolcott
Wolff, Sarah A., 15
Wright, Harriet G. R., 15
Wright, Katherine J., 63
Wright, Nora, 65